Critical Guides to French Texts

38 Ionesco: Rhinocéros

Critical Guides to French Texts

EDITED BY ROGER LITTLE, WOLFGANG VAN EMDEN, DAVID WILLIAMS

IONESCO

Rhinocéros

C.E.J. Dolamore

Lecturer in French
Leeds University

Grant & Cutler Ltd
1984

© Grant & Cutler Ltd
  1984
ISBN 0 7293 0184 2

I.S.B.N. 84-499-7279-5

DEPÓSITO LEGAL: V. 1.323 - 1984

Printed in Spain by
Artes Gráficas Soler, S.A., Valencia
for
GRANT & CUTLER LTD
11 BUCKINGHAM STREET, LONDON W.C.2

Contents

Contents

Note

References to the text of *Rhinocéros* are to the edition in the Collection Folio, Paris: Gallimard, 1977. References to other works are made by quoting in italics the number given to each work in the Selective Bibliography, followed by the page number, thus: *7*, p.21.

'No doubts exist in the herd. Consequently the bigger the crowd the easier it is for an individual to be deluded into thinking he can endure living a lie under the collective umbrella. Nothing illustrates more cogently the way mass movements destroy the individual's sense of responsibility and morality than the comments of leaders of the ... strikers, and the actions they require of their followers.'

(From the leading article, 'Always Somebody Else's Fault', *The Times*, 10 August 1982.)

1. Introduction

When it was first performed, *Rhinocéros* was seen as a turning-point in Ionesco's theatre. For the first time, this champion of pure, or metaphysical, drama, who had for a decade incurred the wrath of writers and critics for whom commitment to the 'real' world was all, had given birth to a play with not only a clear theme, but a political theme into the bargain. To Parisian audiences in January 1960 it seemed that at last Ionesco had committed himself, had a message to convey. What that message was remained open to debate. For some, the dramatist was clearly launching out against totalitarian régimes in general, and in particular the wave of fascism which had given rise to Hitler and the Second World War. For others, it was a less specific attack on mass hysteria, fanatical movements, indeed conformism under any guise. In the midst of the debate, however, there emerged some common accord in recognizing that Ionesco had finally come to consider the human animal as a political being. Some saw this as progress, others as a retreat.

It was clear that, in form and style, *Rhinocéros* was a good deal more sober than Ionesco's earlier works. The dramatist had apparently abandoned the surrealistic dream sequences, the non sequiturs and the out and out contradictions characteristic of his work, for here was an allegorical story with a beginning, middle and end. Ionesco admits that both this play and *Tueur sans gages* (first produced in 1959) 'sont peut-être, malgré moi, un peu moins purement théâtrales, et un peu plus littéraires que les autres' (*13*, p.180). In many cases, his starting point is a conception of theatrical *form* and his plays are the elaboration in dramatic terms, part conscious, part subconscious, of a dream or image. The meaning, or idea, he points out, emerges afterwards. *Rhinocéros*, on the other hand, is the largely conscious development of an *idea*. Several of his plays have originally come into being in the form of short stories; *Rhinocéros* is one of these, the 'nouvelle' being published in 1957. But whereas with *Victimes du devoir*, for instance, which also started life in this way, Ionesco succeeded in reliving the original nightmare while he rewrote it as a play, the construction of *Rhinocéros* was far more lucidly controlled, making it the most conscious and rational of his works to date.

These differences in content and form may well help to explain why *Rhinocéros* marked Ionesco's admission into the theatrical establishment of France, and why it has been his most successful play in terms of the number of productions it has had throughout the world. His earlier plays had been performed in small theatres before diminutive audiences, which had earned their author a reputation as a fairly marginal figure of the avant-garde, and enabled the traditional theatre-going public to keep his challenge to conventional drama at arm's length. But after receiving its world première in Düsseldorf in November 1959, *Rhinocéros* opened at the Théâtre de France in a production by its newly appointed director, Jean-Louis Barrault, on 22 January 1960, and Ionesco was introduced on to the national stage and to a much wider public. Had he therefore been obliged to compromise with the subsidized theatre in order to make his mark?

'J'ai peut-être fait ... certaines concessions' (*13*, p.180), he confesses, but there can be no question of his deliberately adapting his format to suit public taste. He insists that this play, though longer than his others, is 'tout aussi traditionnelle et d'une conception tout aussi classique' (*13*, p.286), a choice of words which illustrates his purist conception of drama. The success of *Rhinocéros* he finds astounding, and suspects people of not understanding it: 'Y voient-ils le phénomène monstrueux de la "massification"? En même temps qu'ils sont "massifiables", sont-ils aussi, et essentiellement, au fond d'eux-mêmes, tous, des individualistes, des âmes uniques?' (*13*, p.292). This certainly does not suggest any major concessions to popular opinion.

In fact, while *Rhinocéros* is different in some respects, the differences are easy to exaggerate. While it was acclaimed as a sign that Ionesco had committed himself politically, he had still not abandoned art to propaganda and was not offering the sort of ideological commitment called for by his most vociferous critics. What is more, the political theme itself was already a recurrent obsession: for instance, the swastika arm-band worn by the Professor in *La Leçon* (an over-explicit symbol, omitted, with the author's approval, when the play was first put on in 1951); or the goose-stepping demagogue, La Mère Pipe, in *Tueur sans gages*. But even in *Rhinocéros* the political theme cannot properly be understood without an appreciation of the metaphysical issues which dominate all Ionesco's writing. The place of man in creation, the whys and wherefores of human life, are questions which have constantly occupied him, in his political essays as well as his dramatic works. The fundamental questions — 'Qu'est-ce que c'est que ce monde? ... Qui suis-je? ... Qu'est-ce que je fais, que fais-je ici, que dois-je faire?' (*14*, p.200) — are those which place all others, whether political, social or everyday, in perspective. These are questions without answers, which plot the limits of human understanding. Set against the mysteries of life itself, man's concern with marginal, socio-political problems seems irrelevant. In *Rhinocéros*, the metaphysical problems come to the fore only at the beginning, but then remain just beneath the surface as a silent commentary on the action. Here, as in life, they are the inevitable basis from which all else springs.

In terms of form, too, the play bears most of the Ionesco hall-marks. Here still are the dehumanized characters and the satire of their mechanical language. Here, too, are the farcical humour and the outlandish surprises. Once more comedy and tragedy form a perplexing and significant alliance. While the story does provide, it is true, a superficially linear development, the play is nevertheless constructed in characteristic Ionesco style, as 'une progression dramatique, une prolifération; un piège qui se resserre sur quelqu'un' (*22*, p.87), with a gradually accelerating rhythm which gives the impression of a world going out of control. In this drama of disintegration, describing 'a downhill plunge', as Pronko has called it (*27*, p.35), man seems to be hurtling towards a black hole of moral extinction from which it is increasingly more difficult to escape. To create this effect, the playwright calls, as usual, upon all the resources of the theatre: set, costumes, props, sound-effects, gesture, movement, and, not least, the device of visible transformation, which occurs in a number of his plays. The one notable element missing here is lighting, which is a major feature in many works and alone creates the opening setting of *Tueur sans gages*. In *Rhinocéros* it is specifically mentioned only at the start of Act I, but its use is clearly called for: one could readily imagine, for example, the ends of Acts II and III becoming progressively darker, bathed in a deepening rhinoceros-green aura, as a sign of the menace closing in around Bérenger.

In this study of *Rhinocéros*, I shall analyse the themes and other aspects within the immediate context of the play and in the light of Ionesco's many writings on life and drama. I shall begin by considering Ionesco's view of the human condition, to which modern writers have given the shorthand title of 'the absurd'. In subsequent chapters, I shall discuss how man's endeavours to cope with his plight are demonstrated by Ionesco to be illusions, nothing but false structures designed to conceal the essential chaos. Finally, by examining the use made of the total language of drama, I shall try to show how form and content combine to create a terrifying image of the dilemma which confronts all of us as individuals.

2. Absurdity, Surprise and Guilt

The concept described by the modern philosophical term, 'the absurd', is probably as old as human life itself. However, in the twentieth century, it has acquired great currency among certain philosophers and writers, to the extent that one could perhaps consider it the watchword of an age. Many theories have been put forward to explain why the particular sense of futility and despair conveyed by the term should have implanted itself so firmly in contemporary consciousness. The spectacular advances of science, the gain in materialistic values and the parallel weakening of religious belief, as well as the unequalled shock and disillusionment created by the outbreak and horrific course of the First World War — these, among other factors in the making of the twentieth century, have contributed to a pervasive sense of the absurdity of life.

Implicit in the philosophy of the absurd is the absence, or 'death', of God, the loss of faith in an absolute which might confer meaning on an otherwise unintelligible destiny. Human existence is seen, therefore, as a meaningless advance towards death, before and beyond which there is only nothingness. In the face of such an absurd fate, man may experience dread or anguish — Heidegger's 'Angst' — and many writers, particularly in France, have devoted their works to creating an acute awareness of this anguish.

Foremost among such literary figures are Malraux, Sartre and Camus, whose major works jointly span, and dominate, the years from the twenties to the fifties. In essays, novels and plays, they illustrate the condition of absurdity which we all share. Each in his own way offers a response to man's destiny, an attempt to make something meaningful out of the nothingness. What distinguishes their successors in the fifties and sixties, the chief exponents of the so-called 'Theatre of the Absurd' (in France, especially Ionesco, Beckett and the early Adamov) is, on the one hand, their use of dramatic form itself as an expression of absurdity, and, on the other, the nihilism, the utter bleakness of their plays. They concentrate, with a grim humour but almost unremitting pessimism, on the anguish of contemplating the sheer pointlessness of all human endeavour.

It is customary to think of Ionesco as being associated with the 'Theatre of the Absurd'. This can be misleading in two ways. Firstly, no such movement exists. The term was coined by the critic, Martin Esslin, in his book of that name (1961) as a convenient heading under which to group a number of twentieth-century dramatists with certain similarities of style and outlook. Secondly, while he may share with many contemporary writers a belief in the senselessness of life, Ionesco does not much favour the use of that fashionable term, 'the absurd'.

More of an agnostic than an atheist, he sees life as having no purpose or meaning that we can fathom. Its pointlessness is constantly brought home to us by the fact that at some unpredictable moment it will be negated by death. 'A quoi bon tout', implores Bérenger in *Tueur sans gages*, 'si ce n'est que pour en arriver là?' (*2*, p.89). Throughout Ionesco's work, the fundamental questions about the mystery of existence recur again and again: '"Qu'est-ce que?..." (Qu'est-ce que cela qui est?), "Pourquoi?" et "Comment?"' (*15*, p.132). What do we live for? Perhaps it is for nothing; or for some purpose beyond our understanding; but whatever answer we give, we remain in total ignorance: 'Ni le "pourquoi absolu" ni le "comment absolu" ne peuvent avoir d'autre réponse que: "je ne sais pas"' (*15*, p.137). All we can do is wander aimlessly towards the only certainty: 'Je meurs, tu meurs, il meurt' (*13*, p.66).

Although he himself uses the term 'absurd' often enough as a convenient shorthand, Ionesco finds it too imprecise and inadequate to define his own outlook, which is more instinctive and emotional than philosophical. The world strikes him above all as strange: 'insolite' and 'étrange' are used throughout his writings to describe it; and his response to it is defined as 'étonnement', 'stupéfaction' or 'hébétude', because he finds existence — the sheer fact of existence — surprising and bewildering. Just as modern physicists explain the fundamental properties of atoms in terms of discontinuous quanta and random transitions, so Ionesco's world, lacking intelligible laws, is unpredictable and illogical. He is continually amazed, whether contemplating the fundamental mysteries of life, or observing man's baffling capacity for cruelty and murder. In a world devoid of necessity, we compound our existential anguish by the addition of our own (self-)destructive power: 'On se tue, on se suicide, justement parce qu'on ne veut pas mourir' (*12*, p.226).

Although he is more commonly identified with a despairing attitude, Ionesco's characteristic state of surprise is in fact ambivalent. His autobiographical works show him oscillating between the two poles of wonder and horror, leaving him with the impression

> d'avoir vécu intensément ces deux sentiments contradictoires: le monde est à la fois merveilleux et atroce, un miracle et l'enfer, et ces deux sentiments contradictoires, ces deux vérités évidentes constituent la toile de fond de mon existence personnelle et de mon œuvre littéraire. (*18*, p.325)

His journals record memories of fleeting states of ecstasy, belonging mainly but not exclusively to his childhood, when the world appeared suddenly to be suffused with light and he experienced a sense of harmony with his surroundings, coupled with a feeling of weightlessness. Fear and anguish were replaced by a childlike wonderment. The fundamental questions did not disappear, but the absence of solutions lost its grimness. The wonder lay in the questions themselves and the mystery was embraced on its own terms: as Marie puts it in *Le Roi se meurt*, 'L'impossibilité de répondre est la réponse même, elle est ton être même qui éclate, qui se répand. Plonge dans l'étonnement et la stupéfaction sans limites' (*4*, p.41). Echoes of such states are not uncommon in his plays. The characters who take flight in *Amédée* and *Le Piéton de l'air*, and the illuminated worlds of *Tueur sans gages* and *La Soif et la faim* evoke this ideal of light and weightlessness.

In *Rhinocéros*, there are faint echoes of these images, albeit cast in a somewhat ironic tone. For instance, the opening of Act I, as described in the text — a Sunday morning under a bright summer sky, filled with the ringing of church bells — bears some resemblance to a description in the autobiographical *Printemps 1939*: 'le moment le plus heureux de ma vie: dimanche matin, les cloches. Printemps. La veille, il avait plu. Le ciel est pur, comme lavé. Un soleil tiède' (*12*, p.193). This childhood memory of a joyful, new-born world is transposed in the play as a haven of complacency: the serenity of the scene is ironically shattered when the bells abruptly fall silent and the banality of the material world breaks through. The two settings, apparently so similar in atmosphere, are actually worlds apart.

Also in Act I, Jean and Bérenger contrast their experiences of life in terms of their sensations of weight. The latter can hardly support his own body, whereas Jean is quite carried away with his lightness: 'Je pèse plus que vous. Pourtant, je me sens léger, léger, léger!' (p.43), and he flaps his arms about as if going to take off. This leads to an amusing collision with the Vieux Monsieur, which brings Jean down to earth again. His defiance of gravity indicates someone at peace with himself and the world, quite free of the burden of anguish which oppresses Bérenger. But Jean floats on a cushion of blindness and indifference; he is buoyed up by ignorance and self-deception. There is irony in his lightness, for it is a sign of his empty-headedness, whereas Bérenger's heaviness is a straightforward symbol of his anguish.

Stripped of irony, the positive pole of Ionesco's 'étonnement d'être' is discernible only fleetingly in Bérenger's love for Daisy in Act III: 'Tant que nous sommes ensemble, je ne crains rien, tout m'est égal! ... Mon amour, ma joie! ma joie, mon amour...' (p.220). But the opposite pole of surprise, that of anguish and horror, is fully illustrated in the character of Bérenger. When we see him at the start of the play, he is suffering from a hangover, a figure of confusion, forgetfulness and bewilderment. During the first half of the act, he mutters disjointedly about being out of place in the world, as if he cannot quite understand what is wrong: 'Non, je ne m'y fais pas,

à la vie' (p.20); 'Des angoisses difficiles à définir. Je me sens mal
à l'aise dans l'existence' (p.42). His headache and his feelings of
discomfort and fatigue represent in physical form his 'difficulté
d'être'. He speaks of bearing 'a burden' (p.43); of life 'weighing
down' on him (p.45); of death being a more natural state than
life (p.46); of being unsure even of his own existence (pp.43, 46).
Living itself seems an unnatural business: 'C'est une chose
anormale de vivre' (p.45).

It is noticeable, however, that, in his dreamy state, Bérenger
does not complain of his lot with the sort of intensity we might
expect. This is because, like Ionesco himself, he attempts to
drown his fears in alcohol: 'Cela me calme, cela me détend,
j'oublie' (p.42). The relief may only be partial and temporary,
but he succeeds up to a point in deadening the horror of contemplating his existence. It indicates, of course, a weakness, not
just that of Bérenger himself, but that of mankind, tainted with
imperfection. Bérenger's drinking carries a symbolic meaning,
as Jean unwittingly indicates: 'Ce n'est pas d'eau que vous avez
soif, mon cher Bérenger...' (p.16). He is about to lecture his
listener on the dangers of alcoholism, but, with dramatic irony,
Ionesco clearly has something else in mind, namely 'la soif
d'absolu', man's yearning for an absolute which his relative
world is unable to provide. Bérenger's unquenchable thirst is a
symbol of his metaphysical alienation and desire.

The effect of his intoxication is double-edged. It dulls his
consciousness and his capacity for surprise, so that while
everyone else is astounded to see the orderly peace of a summer's
day disturbed by a charging rhinoceros, Bérenger himself barely
flinches. There is some truth in Botard's sarcastic comment in
Act II: 'Il a tellement d'imagination! Avec lui, tout est possible'
(p.103). It is as if alcohol gave Bérenger greater access to the
infinite realm of the imagination, so much more in harmony
with the infinitely strange, unpredictable world he inhabits.
Everything being possible, nothing is really surprising.
However, this expansion of the subconscious through alcohol is
achieved only at the expense of consciousness. The 'burden' of
the physical world is eased but takes away with it man's lucidity,
his critical faculty. So Bérenger is left indifferent to the

astonishing events which take place around him. He does not for
the moment experience the shock expressed by his fellows, for
whom the appearance of the rhinoceros is an affront to reason
and order. He thus feels no need to explain the occurrence away
and it is only at Jean's insistence that he offers explanations
which are, to say the least, fanciful and half-hearted — that it
has escaped from a circus, hidden under a stone, nested on a
branch, etc. (p.36). It is only for the sake of friendship that he
conforms to society's need to find reasons, even for the
irrational.

By Act III, the situation has changed. With the nightmare
becoming ever more menacing, Bérenger realizes the importance
of keeping alert and lucid. He now remains relatively sober,
despite the temptations of the brandy bottle, and he observes the
world in all its strangeness. Applying his conscious mind to an
irrational universe, he cannot get over it: 'Moi, je suis surpris, je
suis surpris, je suis surpris! Je n'en reviens pas' (p.184). He
cannot be immune from the shock of discovering that human
beings can willingly turn into monsters, that they can give up
their identities to be swallowed up in a subhuman mass. When
even the anti-rhinoceros, Botard, becomes a rhinoceros,
Bérenger notes with horror: 'Mais alors, alors on peut s'attendre
à tout!' (p.205). Of course, the danger of expecting that
anything can happen is that we can become inured to surprise. It
is tiring and challenging constantly to be taken aback. We may
even start to accept the illogical as if it were logical. What saves
Bérenger from the epidemic is his refusal to be indifferent
(p.184), and his determination to recognize the absurd as
absurd.

He knows that salvation does not lie in blindness and
escapism. When Daisy tells him, 'Evade-toi dans l'imaginaire'
he dismisses the proposal as 'Facile à dire!' (p.227). Besides, the
imagination is not for Ionesco a means of escape, but, on the
contrary, a deepening of consciousness: 'La vérité est dans
l'imaginaire ... L'imagination ne peut mentir. Elle est révélatrice
de notre psychologie, de nos angoisses permanentes ou actuelles,
des préoccupations de l'homme' (*18*, p.176). Bérenger
instinctively realizes that his imagination, his inner life, is what

keeps him human, but it increases, rather than relieves, his torment. As long as his conscious mind, too, remains alert, relatively free from the stupefying effects of alcohol, the fears rising from his subconscious will grow more and more difficult to bear. Painful as it is, he knows that this integrity is vital if he is to resist. He must guard against indifference, and maintain his capacity for horror and surprise.

It is the alternative solution which the others adopt, and this is much less painful. They preserve their illusion of an ordered universe by coming to justify the unjustifiable. Their view of the world cannot accommodate surprise for long, so they erect mental barricades against it:

> DUDARD: Moi aussi, j'ai été surpris, comme vous. Ou plutôt je l'étais. Je commence déjà à m'habituer. (p.184)

> DAISY: On s'y habitue, vous savez. Plus personne ne s'étonne des troupeaux de rhinocéros parcourant les rues à toute allure. Les gens s'écartent sur leur passage, puis reprennent leur promenade, vaquent à leurs affaires, comme si de rien n'était. (p.211)

For everyone except Bérenger, the preservation of a familiar order, however illusory, protects them against 'l'insolite', but in so doing, they lose sight of their humanity. Bérenger, remaining lucid despite the tots of cognac he takes to assuage his fear, never loses his deep-seated awareness that the human must be defended against dehumanization, and the main piece of his armour is his capacity for surprise.

An important theme of *Rhinocéros*, and one which stems from man's metaphysical alienation, is that of guilt. Coe has remarked that 'In Ionesco's 'Man', there is more than a suspicion of original sin' (*24*, p.84). It appears in many of his plays, notably in *Amédée* and *Tueur sans gages*, whose central images have both been defined by the author as 'le péché originel' (*22*, pp.31, 83). In *Rhinocéros*, there are many references, explicit and implicit, to feelings of guilt, mostly Bérenger's. It is a major sign of the emotional inner life which demonstrates his individuality and distinguishes him from the rest.

The whole of the opening scene involves Jean's arousing and aggravating Bérenger's guilt feelings over the complete range of his 'antisocial behaviour', from his lack of punctuality — the arrogant Jean has deliberately arrived late, causing his criticism to backfire, since Bérenger now does not need to feel so bad: 'Alors, je me sens moins coupable' (p.15) — to his lack of interest in the cultural life. We may feel at times that his guilt is misplaced, since it is largely provoked by a laudable inability to conform, such as when he apologizes for arriving late at the office (p.101), or when he humbles himself before Dudard: 'Je n'en doute pas, excusez-moi. Je suis trop anxieux. Je me corrigerai. Je m'excuse aussi de vous retenir, de vous obliger à écouter mes divagations' (pp.187-88). No doubt we react similarly to his shame at being incapable of becoming a rhinoceros: 'J'ai trop honte!' (p.245). However, his guilt is inspired also by finer feelings, notably his regret at having fallen out with Jean — for which he blames himself — and at his quarrel with Daisy — which ends with his slapping her face: 'Oh! pardonne-moi, ma chérie, pardonne-moi!' (p.239). Unworthy as they may be, Bérenger values their companionship enough to take all their guilt upon himself.

It is noticeable that, apart from Bérenger (and Daisy in the final scene), none of the others shows any awareness of guilt. Jean, for instance, makes no concessions to human fallibility, not even when Bérenger points out that he does not practise what he preaches. 'Aucun rapport avec vous', he replies furiously (p.59). The same is true of Dudard, Botard and Papillon, each of whom has a ready answer for everything, purporting to show he is in the right. On the other hand, all of them are more than ready to dispense blame:

BOTARD: C'est votre faute.
DUDARD: Pourquoi la mienne, et pas la vôtre?
BOTARD: Ma faute? C'est toujours sur les petits que ça retombe. (p.117)

If we take original sin to be a sign of man's Fall from grace, and the fundamental cause of his metaphysical anguish, then, if these characters' own testimonies are to be believed, they ought to have one foot in Paradise. But, just as man is flawed, so does he bear responsibility for his imperfections. Thus guilt is inherent in the human condition, and by accepting it — which we can only do as individuals — we show ourselves to be human. Bérenger alone is aware of this: 'Il se trompe. Il est humain', he generously says of Dudard (p.217). He also knows that man cannot always avoid the evil for which he is responsible: 'Parfois, on fait du mal sans le vouloir. Ou bien, on le laisse se répandre' (p.225). Instinctively, Bérenger knows what it means to be human. However, by repressing their guilt, the other characters are denying their humanity. Unlike him, they find no difficulty in living, since, apparently, their consciences are clear. But in fact, subconsciously, they are blinding themselves to the reality of human nature, protesting their innocence on the one hand, and hiding behind a screen of collective amorality on the other. The desire to suppress a sense of personal responsibility by joining the mass — in short, the rush to become rhinoceroses — is a further manifestation of their flight from the truth. In psycho-analytic terms, their rhinoceritis, this 'mal nerveux', as Bérenger calls it (p.179), might be seen as a psychosomatic disorder brought on by the repression of guilt.

The best illustration of the theme of guilt comes in the love-scene between Bérenger and Daisy. They are the sole represent-atives of humanity, the archetypal couple. Theirs is an attempt to rediscover an emotional bond between individuals, in a world where passion is dead and the only unity is in conformism. Bérenger sees them as representing Adam and Eve, with a new chance to 'regenerate the human race' (p.236). But this is the Garden of Eden after the Fall, and, like Adam and Eve before them, they come up against the obstacle of guilt.

Their scene together begins with Bérenger blaming Daisy (and inwardly no doubt himself) for not restraining Dudard: 'Vous auriez dû le retenir de force ... Vous auriez dû être plus ferme' (p.218). Soon, Bérenger is made to feel guilty as he lies about his drinking (p.222). He reproaches Daisy for her treatment of the flirtatious Papillon (p.225), and then himself for his treatment of Jean (p.226). At this point, Daisy takes the initiative in attempting to strip away their feelings of guilt: 'A quoi bon les remords? ... Nous avons tous des fautes, peut-être. Pourtant, toi et moi, nous en avons moins que tant d'autres ... Nous sommes bons, tous les deux.' (pp.226-27). But the quest for innocence can be no more than an illusion, and there is more than a hint of self-deception in what Daisy is proposing:

> DAISY: La culpabilité est un symptôme dangereux. C'est un signe de manque de pureté.
> BERENGER: Ah! oui, cela peut mener à ça ... Beaucoup d'entre eux ont commencé comme ça!
> DAISY: Essayons de ne plus nous sentir coupables. (pp.227-28)

However, it is not so much guilt itself which is dangerous, but rather the repression of guilt, the attempt to ignore it. Moreover, the lack of purity which Daisy mentions recalls man's Fall from grace, a disenchantment which can lead him in search of dangerous, idealistic solutions. The same concept figured in the fascist doctrine of recent times, which led directly to the gas-chambers. The ideals of 'purity' and 'purification' can take on a very ugly aspect when they are made to ride roughshod over human imperfection.

So, try as they might, the couple cannot sustain their precarious sense of innocence for long. They are soon shedding their guilt feelings by accusing each other: 'C'est bien ce que tu voulais. — C'est toi qui le voulais! — C'est toi. — Toi!' (p.232); and immediately, the noise of the rhinoceroses rises as an audible commentary on their disintegration. The final movement of their duet is announced by the renewal of guilt feelings in Daisy — 'C'est peut-être notre faute' — and it is Bérenger's turn to warn of their dangers, echoing her words, and to console her with illusions of human happiness, which, in their present predicament, seem absurdly unconvincing: 'Il ne faut pas avoir de remords. Le sentiment de la culpabilité est dangereux. Vivons notre vie, soyons heureux. Nous avons le devoir d'être heureux' (pp.233-34).

When Daisy finally renounces love, she replaces it by shame: 'J'en ai un peu honte, de ce que tu appelles l'amour, ce sentiment morbide, cette faiblesse de l'homme' (p.239). This is a measure of how far they have fallen from their 'state of grace'. In a sense, it is not just 'vingt-cinq années de mariage' (p.240) that they have lived, but the whole history of love in an imperfect world. Appropriately, amid the mutual insults on which they part, each acknowledges his guilt in the brief moments of reconciliation: 'BERENGER: Excuse-moi; DAISY: Pardonne-moi aussi' (p.242). As Daisy slips away to rid herself of the burden of responsibility which the experience of individuality placed on her, Bérenger remains alone, his own guilt even heavier than before: 'C'est ma faute, si elle est partie ... Encore quelqu'un sur la conscience' (p.243).

This important scene epitomizes man's experience as an individual. He strives for innocence, scarcely believing he is unworthy of it, comes to recognize that guilt is an inherent part of human life, and is faced with an existential choice: to deny guilt and lose his quality as a human individual, or to accept it with all that it implies. I have tried to show how, with the other characters, the absence, or repression, of guilt amounts to a denial of their humanity. In Daisy's case, her brief flirtation with uniqueness brings her an awareness of guilt, but she is not strong enough as an individual to bear the burden; she abdicates her responsibility and escapes into the mass, which has no conscience. Bérenger, too, is tempted by similar pressures, but in the end his deeper understanding of what it means to be human allows him, indeed obliges him, to live with guilt. It is the hall-mark of his condition as a human being and as an individual.

I have considered the theme of guilt at some length because it, more than anything else, acts as a reminder throughout the play of the existential issues raised by Bérenger at the start. Between Act I and Act III, the principal focus of 'l'insolite' shifts from the metaphysical absurd to the equally inexplicable and intolerable activities of man. The appearance of a rhinoceros or two at the beginning may have seemed initially to be no more than further evidence of an incomprehensible universe. But when, in Act II, it transpires that they are actually mutations of a compliant 'homo sapiens', it is clear that humanity has finally given up the unequal struggle with its destiny and joined forces with the absurd. We should, however, be wary of making too sharp a distinction between the metaphysical and political issues, for, as Ionesco has frequently made clear, the two are closely connected: 'Notre conscience sociale découle de notre conscience métaphysique, de notre conscience existentielle' (*18*, p.325). It is precisely because man wanders aimlessly in the darkness that, out of ignorance and desperation, he blunders towards apparent solutions in the social or political context. Beware the self-styled saviours of mankind, Ionesco warns us: 'Quand je vois un bon apôtre, je m'enfuis comme lorsque je vois un dément criminel armé d'un poignard' (*13*, p.229). We desire nothing so much as their utopian solutions, and, unless we are careful, we allow ourselves to be led towards imaginary ideals — ideological systems — which reveal themselves to be only collectivisms, totalitarianisms and tyrannies.

There are, of course, no Utopias. Our world cannot contain any perfect solutions. But our reason is easily dominated by our desire. In his blindness and cruelty, man is a victim of his 'soif d'absolu': 'Les hommes s'entretuent parce que le monde est mal foutu' (*19*, p.19). However, though man may be a helpless puppet, doomed to failure and to death, he remains, for Ionesco, responsible for the evil he does. The only answer to our dilemma, according to Ionesco, lies in our seeing beyond the political issues, which divide us, to the broader issues, which unite us in a common plight.

It is time for me to turn to the more 'committed' themes that come to the fore in *Rhinocéros*, but it is important that they be seen in relation to the wider, fundamental questions which underpin the whole of Ionesco's theatre. Ideologies, clichés, logical and social structures are all barriers erected by man to protect himself from absurdity, but they merely conceal the real issues and exacerbate the dilemma. As Ionesco has said in an interview, 'La politique, l'organisation sociale ... ça nous fait oublier le seul problème authentique, celui de la signification de notre existence ... c'est que nous sommes là dans l'étonnement et que nous sommes faits pour la mort' (*22*, p.160).

3. The Theme of Ideology

Eugène Ionesco was born in Romania in 1912 of a French mother and Romanian father, but was brought up in France until the age of thirteen. Only then did he return to his native land, where he learned Romanian and completed his education, taking a degree in French at Bucharest University. In 1938, when he was twenty-six, he came back to France, where he was to settle, ostensibly to write a thesis on French poetry, but mainly to escape the mounting tide of fascism in Romania. Shortly before leaving Bucharest, he confided these thoughts to his diary:

> Les policiers sont rhinocéros. Les magistrats sont rhinocéros. Vous êtes le seul homme parmi les rhinocéros. Les rhinocéros se demandent comment le monde a pu être conduit par des hommes... Comment faire pour regagner la France. Là, on peut encore se faire comprendre. On a l'impression finalement que ce désir même est coupable. C'est comme un péché de ne pas être rhinocéros... Toutes les armées sont des armées de rhinocéros. Tous les soldats des justes causes sont des rhinocéros. Toutes les guerres saintes sont rhinocériques. La justice est rhinocérique. Les révolutions sont rhinocériques. (*15*, p.114)

Some twenty years separate these comments from the writing of *Rhinocéros*, and a few more years still were to elapse before Ionesco came across these earlier descriptions of the political scene in the 1930s and noted with surprise how they anticipated his play. He had forgotten using the term 'rhinoceros' to describe the mindless fanatics of ideological change, yet somehow the image had imposed itself again when he wanted to evoke the spread of collective hysteria, engulfing the individual conscience.

In the 1930s, Europe, faced with the threat of communism, experienced a terrifying growth of fascism, as national-socialist parties, particularly in Germany, Italy, Spain and Romania, swelled with new recruits and imposed their rule of hatred. Few countries in Europe escaped their influence; France had her 'Action française', while, in Britain, Sir Oswald Mosley's 'blackshirts' terrorized the country's Jewish communities. Everywhere, the nationalist frenzy sought to 'purify' its stock, and its principal victims were the Jews. The history of our century shamefully records how, by 1945, Hitler's Nazi régime had brutally murdered over six million Jewish people.

Ionesco's own experience of these events in his native Romania is not only the primary source of *Rhinocéros*, but also the origin of his vehement opposition to all political ideologies. Throughout the '30s, the Romanian fascist organization, awesomely named the Iron Guard, grew in parallel to Hitler's National-Socialism in Germany, propagandizing, terrorizing all who opposed its creed, and imposing its totalitarian will. In 1940, Romania was occupied by the Germans in their ideological search for 'Lebensraum' (living-space), a euphemism for conquest and domination of Europe. When in 1941, Romania declared war on Russia, this offensive was justified by the need to crush the communist ideology. But three years later, the Red Army expelled the Germans, and Romania found herself occupied again, this time by the Communists, and promptly declared war on Nazi Germany.

The absurdity of this ideological seesaw was epitomized for Ionesco by his father, a Bucharest lawyer, who, thanks to a chameleon-like adaptability, had managed to belong, at the appropriate times, both to the Iron Guard and to the Communist Party. He was, Ionesco explains, one of the few lawyers to be accepted by the new, Soviet-led régime. Yet he insists that his father's actions were not merely sordid opportunism:

> Mon père ne fut pas un opportuniste conscient, il croyait à l'autorité. Il respectait l'Etat. Il croyait à l'Etat quel qu'il fût... Pour lui, dès qu'un parti prenait le pouvoir, il avait

raison. C'est ainsi qu'il fut garde de fer, démocrate franc-
maçon, nationaliste, stalinien. (*15*, p.26)

His was not an isolated case. Like others in Ionesco's family,
and most of his friends, he presented a chronic case of 'rhinoceritis' — 'la rhinocérite de la plupart des gens' (*18*, p.96).
Ionesco has written of friends who, though sharing his
political views, would gradually allow their resistance to fascism
to weaken, such were the pressures to follow mass opinion. 'Of
course', they would insist, 'I don't support the Iron Guard, nor
am I anti-Semitic, but perhaps they have a point when they talk
of purity...', and the germ would eat its way into their minds.
Under the pretext of objective analysis, they would start to make
concessions and expose themselves to contamination. These
were the first classic symptoms, and in a few weeks, the infection
would have spread through their system. In this way, the
original Dudards of the 1930s exchanged their anti-fascism for a
commitment to the Iron Guard, with all the fanaticism of new
converts (*15*, pp.116-17). Such, then, was the climate of those
years, 'lorsque l'intelligentsia devenait peu à peu nazie, anti-
sémite, "Garde de fer"' (*18*, p.94).
It is these first-hand experiences which inspired the political
theme of *Rhinocéros*. That the play should be interpreted, at
least in the first instance, as an attack on fascism, there can be
no doubt: 'Le propos de la pièce a bien été de décrire le
processus de la nazification d'un pays' (*13*, p.286). Certain
features of the text point to this quite clearly. For instance, Jean
is obsessed by health (p.143), argues in favour of strength
(p.149) and naturalness (p.159), and calls for a return to
'l'intégrité primordiale' (p.159). These are specific echoes of
fascist doctrine, with its preoccupation with the will to power
and its ideal of a robust and natural purity. In Act III, Dudard
repeats many of the same arguments, and reminds us, with his
'objective' analysis, of Ionesco's accounts of his friends
allowing the first germs to develop:

Ils ne vous attaquent pas. Si on les laisse tranquilles, ils
vous ignorent. Dans le fond, ils ne sont pas méchants. Il y

a même chez eux une certaine innocence naturelle, oui; de la candeur. (p.183)

Furthermore, the rhinoceroses' green skins are a reminder of the green shirts worn by the Iron Guard legionaries, a point which did not go unnoticed when the play was performed in Romania in 1964, the first of Ionesco's plays to be produced in that country. In the same way, Parisian audiences were inevitably reminded of the green uniforms worn by the Nazi occupiers in 1940.

However marked these references to fascism may be, the play in fact calls for a much broader interpretation. Ionesco himself has defined its theme in more general terms as 'les idéologies, devenues idolâtries, les systèmes automatiques de pensée' (*13*, p.287). Indeed, he no longer sees Nazism as a major threat to human liberty, its place having been taken by the similarly conformist, oppressive and totalitarian doctrine of communism. Remembering how Romania, in the 1940s, came under the yoke of tyrannies of both right and left, he aims his attack at all such collectivist régimes which subordinate the freedom of the individual to some generalized abstraction, such as Society, State, Nation or Race. In 1967, he wrote: 'A ce moment, je parlais de la mentalité fasciste et des Gardes de fer et de leur collectivisme. Aujourd'hui, cela s'appliquerait aux marxistes et aux sociétés marxistes' (*15*, p.116)

In fact, Ionesco allows the spectator considerable freedom of interpretation, a freedom which all too often appears to have been spurned through the desire to particularize. Whereas, in his original Paris production, Barrault left no doubt about the play's significance for him by accompanying the performance with songs of the German army, its meaning need not always be limited to this. One critic writes:

Ainsi, les Allemands ont vu, dans *Rhinocéros*, une charge contre le nazisme; les Anglais, contre le communisme; les Français, contre l'autoritarisme de 'de Gaulle'; les Américains, contre l'automatisme; ceux d'au-delà du Rideau de Fer, contre le capitalisme. (*23*, pp.125-26)

We may wonder to what extent these assertions are accurate, but it is clear that the play may mean different things to different people. On the other hand, in Russia, where it has been published in translation but not performed, Ionesco explains that he was asked to reduce the ambiguity in order to avoid confusion — they only wanted rhinoceroses of the right. 'Mais', he adds, 'les rhinocéros sont partout' (*18*, p.99).

As we widen the lens through which we examine Ionesco's theme, we begin to focus, not only on the specific doctrines of fascism and communism, but on a great many ideologies, both political and religious. Ionesco has a profound mistrust of *all* ideologies, fixed systems of thought which demand conformity, and are apt to be violently intolerant of dissension. The loftiness of their utopian ideals may be used to justify the wildest crimes. The vigour of Ionesco's views on this subject can be witnessed from the following extract from an article written in 1959:

> Il me semble que de notre temps et de tous les temps, les religions ou les idéologies ne sont et n'ont jamais été que les alibis, les masques, les prétextes de cette volonté de meurtre, de l'instinct destructeur, d'une agressivité fondamentale, de la haine profonde que l'homme a de l'homme; on a tué au nom de l'Ordre, contre l'Ordre, au nom de Dieu, contre Dieu, au nom de la patrie, pour défaire un Ordre mauvais... Les sauveurs de l'humanité ont fondé les Inquisitions, inventé les camps de concentration, construit les fours crématoires, établi les tyrannies. (*13*, pp.228-29)

Although there are no murders in *Rhinocéros* (except for that of the cat — an evil omen, treated in burlesque style), the play illustrates the necessary preliminaries to the 'purges' mentioned above, and we are made fully aware of the menace presented by the rhinoceroses, of their violence and destructiveness.

It is important to note that Bérenger does not oppose their ideology with any alternative doctrine of his own, only an intuitive belief in the uniqueness of human individuality. To do otherwise would be to imply that one ideology were better than another, which is not at all what Ionesco believes. As an upholder of individual freedom, he presents his play as an indictment of all ideologies, of rhinoceritis in all its forms.

What, then, are the symptoms of this 'sickness', according to Ionesco's diagnosis? The use of the ill-starred rhinoceros as a symbol of moral corruption immediately suggests a number of superficial features: unwieldy, brutish, ugly, armour-plated and with a fearsome horn (or horns) jutting out from its nose, this 'animal terrible, borné, qui fonce droit devant lui' (*18*, p.95) is a perfect image of mindless destructiveness. What is more, one rhinoceros looks very much like another, so that those who see the first of them cannot be sure about its one distinguishing feature — the number of horns on its nose. Dudard is soon lost in the crowd (p.218), while, as an amusing touch, the Logician remains recognizable by the boater impaled on his horn (p.200).

In an interview, Ionesco expressed minor misgivings about his choice of symbol. Rhinoceroses, it seems, do not herd together, an essential feature of the collectivist spirit inspiring the transformations. A more accurate term, he suggested, might have been 'mouton féroce' (*18*, p.95), for it is precisely the sheep-like, follow-my-leader instinct which is important here. Clearly, though, such a familiar image would have been less grotesque; the rhinoceros is at once more monstrous, more terrifying, and (from a safe distance) more humorous.

Even before the first beast has announced its presence, the play has already introduced us to a primary symptom of the disease. Jean's diatribe against Bérenger's non-conformism, concerning punctuality, dress and petty-bourgeois virtues (sobriety, will-power, duty, etc.) shows the traits of the pachyderm in all but physical form. The thick-skinned resistance to personal responsibility and the values Jean upholds are those of the collectivity; they have no meaning for the individual beyond that context. Conformism is not only a virtue ('Tout le monde travaille et moi aussi, moi aussi comme tout le monde'), it is a duty ('Tout le monde doit s'y faire'), and anyone who ignores this rule is subjected to ridicule: 'Seriez-vous une nature supérieure?' (p.20). Jean represents the conformist ethos, the unthinking adoption of ready-made ideas. 'Le rhinocéros', as Ionesco tells us, 'c'est l'homme des idées reçues' (*18*, p.94).

Yet there is something still more sinister about Jean, implied by his fits of rage (heralding the charging rhinos) and by his authoritarian, dogmatic manner. He knows what is right and accepts no contradiction: 'Je pense ce qui est' (p.38); 'Je ne dis jamais de sottises, moi!' (p.70). His bigoted glorification of conformism carries distant echoes of Hitler's 'One people, one empire, one leader', as the desire to conform becomes the desire to compel others to conform, backed up by a display of force. Jean's closed mind is fertile pasture for the rhinoceritis virus, and Ionesco deliberately chooses this instantly recognizable social type to be the first one visibly to undergo transformation. If there is an evolution in his character, it is that one fixed set of ideas gives way to another, and social conformism to ideological conformism. In Act I, he observes (twice) of the rhinoceros: 'Il fonce droit devant lui' (pp.23, 61); he might easily have been speaking of himself. In Act II, he is speaking of himself when he cries: 'J'ai un but, moi. Je fonce vers lui' (p.152). The tyranny inherent in him has now grown to the full, the blustering caricature of Act I has turned into a ferocious monster, and woe betide anyone who stands in his way: 'Je te piétinerai, je te piétinerai' (p.164).

We can see, therefore, that the image of the rhinoceros does not in itself represent a particular ideological stance. It is, like all the physical elements of Ionesco's theatre, the symbol of a state of mind, a visual projection of the inner world. It expresses in dramatic terms the absence of human values and, particularly, of individuality. It is what remains when we abdicate our humanity, when we replace our faculties of thought and feeling with a system of ready-made ideas. The conformist, by the suppression of individuality, already carries the virus of rhinoceritis in him and lays himself open to the contagious power of ideological propaganda. This activates the virus and it spreads like a cancer of the mind.

It should be stressed that, in terms of the medical metaphor which Ionesco uses throughout the play and elsewhere, *Rhinocéros* concerns, not simply a disease, but an epidemic. It illustrates an accelerating process, the spread of ideological contagion. It is this that gives the play its dramatic power, its nightmare effect. Ionesco's point is that once we abandon our identities in favour of conformist anonymity, we easily fall prey to mass movements. When we stop thinking for ourselves, we readily adopt the slogans of propaganda. Once set in motion, the process will, of necessity, gain momentum, as we continue to flee from personal responsibility — the need to think and feel and answer for the consequences — to lose ourselves in the crowd. Expanded and multiplied in this way, Ionesco's central image evokes the growth of mass hysteria, of collective fanaticism, of what he calls 'psychoses meurtrières collectives' (*15*, pp.170-71), in which we can recognize the psychology of the crowd, guiltless and barbarous.

4. The Corruption of Language

Conformism of thought amounts to an absence of thought. This is illustrated throughout Ionesco's theatre by the vast majority of his characters, with the partial exception of a few questioning individuals, notably the Bérenger figure who appears in different guises in a number of the plays of this period. One feature above all which links the bulk of his characters is the way in which they use language.

A common misconception concerning Ionesco's outlook needs to be clarified at the outset: his drama is not about the impossibility of communication. He rejects 'l'incommunicabilité', because all that can be thought, he claims, is communicable. Sometimes communication is difficult, but never impossible. Of course, there are whole areas of our experience — the fundamental questions about the nature of our existence — which defy expression. This is so, as we have already seen, because such problems are beyond our understanding, and we can only express them as questions, not answers. But within our human limitations, we do manage to communicate with one another. It would be pointless, after all, for a dramatist and essayist to write, if he did not believe others would understand him: 'Un auteur, par définition, est quelqu'un qui croit à l'expression' (22, p.124). Indeed, Ionesco finds it amazing that people can understand one another: 'Ils se parlent. Ils se comprennent. C'est cela qui est stupéfiant' (22, p.59).

Such childlike wonder at the very existence of language fades, however, and turns to horror, when language is used, not to reveal truth, but to conceal it:

Je crois que la communication est possible, sauf si on la refuse pour toutes sortes de raisons: mauvaise foi, manque d'attention, passion politique, incompréhension temporaire... C'est que les systèmes d'expression ne servent pas

toujours à communiquer, ils servent souvent à cacher une
pensée. Les idéologies généralement sont des alibis et
dissimulent, volontairement, bien autre chose que ce
qu'elles avouent. (*22*, p.124)

The characters of Ionesco's plays only fail to communicate
either because they do not want to, or because they have created
for themselves a mechanical, impersonal world, devoid of
individual psychology. The latter, especially, is the case in early
plays such as *La Cantatrice chauve* (whose characters Ionesco
describes as 'des rhinocéros du centre' *18*, p.99) and it is still
valid for *Rhinocéros*, albeit in less extreme form. Throughout
his plays, the characters illustrate a divorce between two of
man's most precious faculties, speech and thought: 'Les person-
nages de mes pièces sont des gens qui prononcent des slogans ce
qui leur épargne la peine de penser' (*22*, p.124).

There is, therefore, a distinction to be made between non-
communication, caused by man's having given up the power to
think as an individual, and the impossibility of breaking through
the metaphysical silence which surrounds us. As with metaphysics and politics, however, the distinction is not clear-cut,
since one is a product of the other. One possible reaction to our
existential anguish is for us to shut our minds to it, resigning
ourselves instead to 'la paresse mentale qui nous cache
l'étrangeté du monde' (*13*, p.60). But if we shrink from thought
for fear of what it may reveal, we lose the essence of our
humanity; we become hollow and allow the outer void to
penetrate our being. Alternatively, we can, like Ionesco himself,
carry on thinking and expressing our thoughts, fears and
anguish. In this way, we resist the void, like Bérenger at the end
of the play. Ultimately, for all of us, the void will triumph, but
we should deny our humanity and become accomplices of the
absurd if we gave up the struggle, as the other characters of
Rhinocéros have done.

In Act III, Bérenger makes a telling assessment of his fellow
men when he says to Dudard: 'Si les dirigeants et nos con-
citoyens pensent tous comme vous, ils ne se décideront pas à
agir' (p.187). Like Jean, who advises one thing and does

another, and like all the characters who simply flow with the tide, Dudard is a man of words rather than actions. By far the greater part of *Rhinocéros* concerns the art of talking and of saying nothing. Words are used as an antidote to reality — they fill the void, but only with their own emptiness. By constant discussion and debate, the characters try to insure themselves against silence and the contemplation of their human plight. In fact, since their words are without substance, a mere alibi for thought, and only of value for their noise, the characters are engaged in the most illusory escapism. Because they have repudiated language as communication between one individual consciousness and another, the more they talk, the more barren their inner lives become.

Most of the dialogue in the play is made up of clichés, platitudes and slogans. The stale, second-hand language serves as a vehicle for stale, second-hand thoughts. The distinctive human quality of language has been discarded; it has become ossified and mechanical, conveying no more meaning than the trumpeting of rhinoceroses. There are so many examples of platitude in the play — for the most part highly amusing when they are served up as the pinnacle of human wisdom — that a few must suffice as illustration:

> Plus on boit, plus on a soif, dit la science populaire. (p.16)
> C'est pas comme les jeunes d'aujourd'hui. (p.31)
> La vie est une lutte, c'est lâche de ne pas combattre. (p.48)
> C'est comme la religion qui est l'opium des peuples. (p.106)
> Ne jugez pas les autres, si vous ne voulez pas être jugé. (p.184)
> Puisqu'il en est ainsi, c'est qu'il ne peut en être autrement. (p.186)

Fossilized language like this is shown to be a touchstone of conformism, as it throws a shroud of uniformity over the uniqueness of personality. Where words do not express our inner being, language, for Ionesco, is in a state of crisis: 'En effet, la pensée est expression de l'être, elle coïncide avec l'être. On peut parler

sans penser. Il y a pour cela à notre disposition les clichés, c'est-
à-dire les automatismes' (*14*, p.48).

The crisis is a grave one, but it provides one of the main
sources of Ionesco's humour. The tragi-comic effects of mindless conversation are exploited in many different forms here.
There is, for example, the standardized response to the appearance of the rhinoceros in Act I: 'Ça alors!' (echoed by all except
Bérenger) in the first instance, and 'Oh! un rhinocéros!',
followed by 'Ça alors!' and 'Oh!' (each repeated several times)
in the second. As with so many of the banalities in the play,
much of their humour derives from the inadequacy of the words
to the seriousness of the situation.

Leaving aside for the moment the main significance of the
Logician's discourse on the syllogism in Act I, it is worth
examining how his conversation with the Vieux Monsieur
becomes entwined in that between Jean and Bérenger. The two
dialogues echo each other in word and sense on several
occasions, each acting as a sort of commentary on the other,
until they are superimposed on each other with Bérenger's and
the Vieux Monsieur's 'C'est compliqué' (p.50). For some time,
they continue to duplicate each other more or less exactly.
Thereupon, they drift slowly apart, come together again like
voices in counterpoint, and finally join forces with 'Qu'est-ce
que vous dites?' (p.59), which heralds the massed chorus of 'Oh!
un rhinocéros!' (pp.60-61). This extremely funny scene is a skil-
fully orchestrated set-piece, pouring scorn on a language so
depersonalized as to drown the individual in the mass. Words
have become as impersonal as coinage, used as a means of barter
in the collective flea-market of worn-out ideas.

Repetition is a device frequently employed by Ionesco to illustrate the 'crisis of language'. It is not unusual for him to repeat
whole scenes where different characters speak the same lines, as
in *L'Impromptu de l'Alma*, or in *Macbett*, where the echoing
speeches indicate the similarity of opposite tyrannies. In
Rhinocéros, Act III opens in almost identical fashion to the
preceding tableau, the visual symmetry of the set being
reinforced by the parallelism of the dialogue, with Dudard
announcing his arrival at Bérenger's door with the same words

as those used by Bérenger when he visited Jean. Social intercourse has become a mechanical affair, and its language conventional and automatic.

Allied to this, is the duplication of names in Act II, tableau II. The old man answers Bérenger's call because he, too, is called Jean. Ionesco underlines the confusion to comic effect by making both the old man's wife, and then Bérenger, call out to their respective 'Jean' (p.138). A similar point is made earlier by Bérenger's accidental pun: 'J'étais à côté de mon ami Jean!... Il y avait d'autres gens' (p.103). Ionesco obviously enjoys this procedure; he often has several characters in a single play bearing the same name, the most memorable case being the whole family of Bobby Watsons described in *La Cantatrice chauve*. When even a name becomes impersonal, language is impotent to express individuality.

With language stripped of its vigour in these various ways, it lends itself easily to manipulation by despots, who reinvigorate it with a meaning of their own. One form which this takes is that of the generalization presented as self-evident truth, the trenchant statement of baseless fact which lends respectability to prejudice and seems to brook no contradiction. The master of this form is Botard, whose borrowed slogans, though devoid of thought, nevertheless have the menacing ring of axiom: 'Les journalistes sont tous des menteurs' (p.94); 'Les Méridionaux ont trop d'imagination' (p.96); 'Les universitaires sont des esprits abstraits qui ne connaissent rien à la vie' (p.101); etc. Such conversation-stopping banalities caricature the totalitarian slogans of hatred.

Behind the comedy inspired by Ionesco's parody of speech, there lie disturbing implications of a world governed by automatons ('human' ones — more dangerous than machines), where individual responsibility and judgement are programmed and institutionalized, as with the bureaucrat or the soldier who is 'only doing his duty'. *Rhinocéros* goes further than earlier plays in taking account of such implications and showing how the commonplace may take on more sinister overtones. Whereas *La Leçon* demonstrated the ominous power of language, with the teacher gradually reducing his pupil to submission by using words as instruments of torture, and finally stabbing her to death with the word 'couteau', it is in *Rhinocéros* that we find the vacuum left behind by thought being filled by a set of ideological slogans. For example, the more rhinocerotic Jean becomes, the more demagogic is his language, full of emotionally charged phrases and a simple rhetoric reminiscent of many a political rally:

> La morale! Parlons-en de la morale, j'en ai assez de la morale, elle est belle la morale! Il faut dépasser la morale ... La nature a ses lois. La morale est antinaturelle ... Il faut reconstituer les fondements de notre vie. Il faut retourner à l'intégrité primordiale. (p.159)

While the cliché diminishes language, the slogan distorts it and turns it into an ideological cudgel.

It is with such a weapon that Bérenger is attacked by Jean and Dudard. They speak of 'nature', 'duty' and 'rights', rabble-rousing slogans with no clearly defined meanings. Jean insists that to emulate 'l'homme supérieur', one must do one's duty. Asked to be more precise, he adds 'son devoir d'employé par exemple' (p.21). Thus the individual is to be reduced to a function, his uniqueness sacrificed to a social role. In Jean's view, rhinoceroses have the same rights as people: 'les rhinocéros ... ont droit à la vie au même titre que nous' (p.158). The word carries all before it; its effect is to trigger an automatic response and anaesthetize thought. Dudard, who criticizes Botard for speaking in clichés and lacking 'arguments précis et objectifs' (p.193), is himself a victim of his own slogans: 'Tout le monde a le droit d'évoluer' (p.205); 'Mon devoir est de ne pas les abandonner, j'écoute mon devoir' (p.217). Yet it is with the same vocabulary that Daisy and Bérenger defend their humanity: 'Alors, nous avons le droit de vivre' (p.227); 'Nous avons le devoir d'être heureux' (pp.233-34). Such all-purpose terms, though they have no more meaning than commonplaces, appear to contain a persuasive degree of moral truth, and therein lies their danger.

The play contains several examples of such language,

especially empty, abstract words, which are thrust like banners into the moral void. There is Jean's triumphant call for 'volonté' (p.20); it seduces Bérenger who, in the last act, enlists its aid against drunkenness (p.170) and rhinoceritis (p.180). Not surprisingly, it can serve both sides of the argument, just as 'volonté' can be 'bonne' or 'mauvaise'. Similarly, both Bérenger (pp.184, 187) and Dudard (p.211) can speak of 'solidarité'. When it comes to tolerance, we tend to consider it a virtue, but should we tolerate evil? Dudard may at first appear to have right on his side when he reproaches Bérenger for being intolerant, while the latter retorts: 'Vous êtes trop tolérant, trop large d'esprit!' (p.194). Bérenger himself is easily confounded when his own slogans are turned against him: 'humanisme', 'l'esprit' (p.161), 'le mal' (p.187), 'anormal' (p.195). Bérenger continues to cling to the power of words — 'J'enverrai des lettres aux journaux, j'écrirai des manifestes, je solliciterai une audience au maire' (p.186) — until in the end they fail him altogether. Bérenger cannot hope to win the verbal battle, not only because he is less intellectual than his opponent, but because words are so easily corrupted.

The language of ideologies is perfectly familiar, only its meaning has changed, confusing the opposition by giving evil an heroic face:

> Regardez-les; écoutez-les: ils ne se vengent pas, ils punissent. Ils ne tuent pas, ils se défendent: la défense est légitime. Ils ne haïssent pas, ils ne persécutent pas, ils rendent justice. Ils ne veulent pas conquérir ni dominer, ils veulent organiser le monde. Ils ne veulent pas chasser les tyrans pour prendre leur place, ils veulent établir l'ordre vrai. Ils ne font que de saintes guerres. (*15*, p.75)

In the same way, in Nazi Germany, the homely word 'völkisch' implied not only 'pure German', but also 'anti-Semitic', and 'System' was a term of abuse for the nature-loving Nazis, though they created a vast filing-system for wanted persons. Thinking of Ionesco's central image, we may remember that 'Schar' ('herd') was the name given to a platoon, while a company or unit rejoiced under the name of a natural phenomenon, 'Sturm' ('storm'). Much the same sort of linguistic approval is given to the rhinoceroses, by insisting on their strength, naturalness, single-mindedness, energy and innocence. In Bérenger's final speech, his moral uncertainty leads him to invest them with 'language' and 'song'; they have 'charm' and they are 'beautiful', while he is 'a monster' (pp.244-45). These are signs, not only that his eyes and ears are deceiving him, but that language itself is corrupt.

In this scene, we witness the final breakdown of language, distorted to the point of disintegration. When Bérenger is left alone, cut off from the world even by radio and telephone, he realizes that communication is impossible between the thinking individual and the dehumanized mass. They speak different languages. The last few moments of the play may appear (especially to the reader) to be simply a monologue by Bérenger. Yet it may not be too eccentric to consider it as a dialogue — a dialogue of the deaf — in which we hear the two languages side by side, Bérenger's and the rhinoceroses'. When he tries to learn their language, the effect is merely grotesque: 'Les hurlements ne sont pas des barrissements' (p.245). The gulf of non-communication can no longer be bridged.

Throughout Ionesco's presentation of the stereotypes of language, there is an element of parody, the humour of which may, at times, conceal the seriousness of his intention. For Ionesco, comedy and tragedy are inseparable. Both are to be found in the drama of the theatre as in the drama of life, not side by side, but one in the other. On the whole, he feels that comedy, 'étant intuition de l'absurde' (*13*, p.61), expresses the desperation of man's plight better than tragedy. Satire, therefore, is not his chief concern. His principal aim remains to express the human condition and man's attempts to cope with it.

By his use of language, man may face or deny the problems of his existence, defend or renounce his humanity. As the manifestation of his thought, language offers him strength and dignity in his struggle with fear and ignorance. But by reducing language to a meaningless set of formulae, man relinquishes an important asset and covers himself in absurdity. His situation is both tragic and derisory. The humour of Ionesco's treatment of this reveals the underlying tragedy while providing the necessary objectivity by which we may laugh. As we laugh at the words we hear on stage, we laugh by implication at ourselves. Although the clichés and slogans we hear in *Rhinocéros* are grossly exaggerated, we can recognize them as the language of our world, the platitudes we hear around us, and perhaps even the ones we use ourselves. By the merest twist, they may become the weapons of ideology, and while Ionesco does not accuse us of deliberately distorting language, he does warn us of the dangers inherent in the dehumanized language of convention.

5. Logic and Learning

The distortion of language is given a last, lethal twist by its use
as a vehicle for a crumbling system of logic. Logic depends on
language to pursue its aims, but when the latter is as hollow and
treacherous as it is here, logic itself can only be a mystification
and a tyranny.

Needless to say, in Ionesco's view of the world as strange and
bewildering, there is little room for rational explanation. A universe governed by the irrational and the inexplicable is a field of
inquiry less for logic than for the science of 'Pataphysics.[1] We
tend to assume that we can best understand our world by
adopting a scientific approach based on logical processes of
thought, and anything which cannot be assimilated by our
reason, we prefer to discount. It is an unsatisfactory procedure,
since the very facts of existence and death (though their
processes can be explained by science) are beyond reason. Logic
and reason are also ill-equipped to deal with whole areas of our
experience: the subconscious world of our dreams and desires,
our loves and fears, our faith. By limiting ourselves to reason,
we limit our understanding.

'La logique', says Ionesco, 'c'est la surface de la conscience.
Le rêve c'est la conscience profonde, substantielle' (*22*, p.77).
Dreams, the natural realm of the subconscious, the imagination
and the irrational, are, however, of vital importance to him.
They are 'plus objectifs que toute pensée' (*18*, p.280) and, for all
their apparent incoherence, they reveal more truth than reason
can ever do. They are the stuff of life itself, for, as Bérenger
says, 'La vie est un rêve' (p.35). Jean's commonplace jibe, 'Vous
rêvez debout!' (p.34), comes closer to the truth than he realizes,

[1] This science of the absurd, which, according to its founder, Alfred Jarry
(1873-1907), stands as far beyond metaphysics as metaphysics is beyond physics,
differs from conventional science in that it discovers laws governing the
exception rather than the rule. Its province is the imagination, not reason.
Ionesco has long been a member of the latter-day Collège de 'Pataphysique, in
which he holds the title of 'Transcendant Satrape'.

since Bérenger *is* a dreamer in the sense that he is aware of an inner world and a deeper level of reality. Jean, meanwhile, 'ne rêve jamais' (p.145), insanely denying the irrational. Such a denial, Ionesco affirms, is tantamount to madness: 'Ceux qui ne rêvent pas sont fous' (*22*, p.121). One form of such madness is, of course, rhinoceritis.

Although, on the other hand, he has some harsh things to say about man's reliance on logic, Ionesco is far from suggesting that no part of the world is rational, or that there is no field where logic may be of use. Indeed, most of his non-dramatic writings are broadly based on the principles of logical discourse. What is at issue in *Rhinocéros* is, firstly, the belief that logical reasoning can provide answers to virtually any question the world may ask of us, and, secondly, the way in which logic is distorted, turned on its head, and finally destroyed, in a blind attempt to explain the inexplicable.

As we have seen, the characters spend most of their time talking, though they have nothing to say. They also conduct their conversations as if everything were based on a simple process of cause and effect: the world is an orderly place; things happen, therefore reasons must be found. The greater part of the text is given over to dialectics; rational argument, like the general hubbub of chatter, provides a defence mechanism against the irrational. Its armour-plating of calm detachment protects the characters from having to react emotionally to the surprises of life. When the first rhinoceroses appear, they cocoon themselves in 'rational' discussion, which saves them from having to face the real problem which does not lend itself to reasoned argument. The endless discussions about the number of horns owned by Asian and African rhinoceroses, the Logician's intervention — which at first seems to be about to bring everyone back to sanity ('là n'est pas la question', p.80), but only leads them further into madness — and the countless other side-issues which occupy the characters, are all ways of staying secure within the structure of a familiar, logical world. Their grief and indignation over the cat's violent death (p.87), the implications of which they fail to see, make an ironic comment on the maximum degree of their emotional involvement. Only to this degree, apparently, is reason prepared to compromise with imagination.

It is no accident that the theme of logic is closely connected with that of learning and culture. The weakness of Bérenger's defence in the war of words is due in part to his intellectual inferiority to his opponents. Yet it is also a strength that his position depends, not on scholarly detachment, as in Dudard's case, but on what he at first calls instinct (illustrating his lack of debating skill), then hastily alters to intuition (p.198). He is not at home with reason because his case is not based on reason. He simply feels that human qualities are superior to the brute strength of the mass. This recalls quite clearly Ionesco's memories of Romania in the thirties. Of the moral resistance of a few individuals to the contagion of fascism, he wrote: 'C'était un refus spontané de tout notre être. Pas tellement intellectuel', adding that his own reaction was 'presque instinctive' (18, pp.96-97). But those who, thanks to their intellectual object-ivity, talked themselves into joining the movement, he described as 'les professeurs de faculté, les étudiants, les intellectuels' (18, p.95). Fascism appealed, not only to men of little learning (like Hitler, for example), but especially to scientists and philo-sophers — the intelligentsia — who helped to give it credibility. What leaves people like Dudard and the Logician prone to contagion is, firstly, their lack of personal involvement, thanks to objectivity and, hence, indifference; and, secondly, their ability to justify their conformism by the use of a spurious, but highly respected, logic. In short, they rationalize their actions.

The importance of these allied themes of logic and learning is emphasized by the prime position occupied in the first act by the hilarious discussion between the Logician and the Vieux Monsieur. The professional thinker, displaying remarkable academic detachment from the terrifying scene they have just witnessed, proceeds to explain the principles of the syllogism. This ancient form of reasoning works by formulating two pro-positions (major and minor premises), joined by a common term, and drawing a necessary conclusion from them. If $A = B$, and $C = A$, therefore $B = C$; hence, all men are mortal, I am a man, therefore I am mortal. The system epitomizes the mathematical clarity of logical reasoning — 'A condition de ne pas en abuser' (p.45), as the Logician ironically points out. However, by muddling his middle term, he contrives to prove that Socrates is a cat, and Ionesco completes the debunking of logic with the Vieux Monsieur's rejoinder, 'C'est vrai, j'ai un chat qui s'appelle Socrate' (p.46). Logic is not only a rigid tool, easily misapplied, it can also be pernicious in its plausibility.

However, as I explained in the previous chapter, this discussion cannot be considered as a separate entity. It is interwoven with the conversation between Jean and Bérenger, on which it provides a highly amusing and derisive commentary. The closest literary parallel is perhaps to be found in the 'Comices agricoles' scene in Flaubert's *Madame Bovary*, where Rodolphe's amorous overtures to Emma are continually shot down by the announcement of prizes for farming. Both scenes are masterpieces of ironic juxtaposition. While the 'intellectual' Logician is expounding on the wonders of logic, Jean is trying to instil into Bérenger the value of 'la culture' and 'l'intelligence' (p.50) — a month's work! — and of a logical approach to life (p.45), even adapting the famous Cartesian *cogito* to his purposes: 'Pensez, et vous serez' (p.46).

A thread of didacticism runs through the play, from Jean and the Logician, by way of the 'ancien instituteur', Botard, to the graduate of law, Dudard. All are eager to impart their knowledge to others, about the right way to set about things, and the proper methods of reasoning. They are, in fact, dictators of thought. It is particularly in the Logician and Dudard, the 'intellectuals', that Ionesco concentrates his attack on logic and learning. Broadly speaking, Dudard occupies a similar position in Act III to that taken by his counterpart in Act I. Both are engaged in casting a smoke-screen of words, logic and erudition over irrational events, and in this, Dudard's sophistry is no less absurd than the Logician's syllogistry. His marvellously obscure response (recalling an old, grammatical chestnut) to Bérenger's question, 'Et les rhinocéros, c'est de la pratique, ou de la théorie?', is the equal of anything in Act I:

DUDARD: L'un et l'autre.

BERENGER: Comment l'un et l'autre!
DUDARD: L'un et l'autre ou l'un ou l'autre. C'est à
débattre! (p.197)

For Dudard, the man of words, the events are a wonderful
opportunity for debate. He would rather talk than come to any
conclusion: 'On doit discuter' (p.197); 'Quelle occasion de
savantes controverses!' (p.214). By failing to involve himself
emotionally, he drifts along the meanderings of his reasoning —
there is nothing really wrong with them; rhinos are innocent and
natural creatures; all the best people have changed; and you can
only judge the experience from within — finally to be swallowed
up in the sea of monsters. At the start, he has no more idea than
Bérenger how the epidemic has come about, but that does not
worry him. He is quite sure that, with the correct, rational
approach, he can keep intact his faith in a logical universe: 'Cela
existe, donc cela doit pouvoir s'expliquer' (p.176). With his
'openness of mind' — which we might think of rather as an
emptiness — he does not feel threatened. The key to coping with
a world full of surprises is apparently to rationalize everything:
'Tout est logique. Comprendre, c'est justifier' (p.194). So, for
Dudard, the universe is still in order, and by 'understanding' the
phenomenon, which amounts, in fact, to a refusal to be
surprised, he comes to accept it. He has no resistance, so he
succumbs.

Jean and Botard, though less erudite than the intellectuals,
make an equal pretence of logic and wisdom. Jean dismantles
Bérenger's fanciful suggestions as to the origin of the rhinoceroses with a humourless logic (p.36), and automatically rejects
the irrational: 'Je ne rêve jamais... Moi, inconsciemment? Je
suis maître de mes pensées' (p.145). When he has to cope with
the shock of seeing his first rhinoceros, it is enough for him to
side-track the issue, reducing a large, irrational problem to a
more conventional, more manageable one:

il [est] dangereux de laisser courir un rhinocéros en plein
centre de la ville, surtout un dimanche matin, quand les
rues sont pleines d'enfants... et aussi d'adultes ... à l'heure
du marché, encore. (p.39)

When the event is repeated, he draws a veil of pretentious erudition over it by initiating the debate about the rhinoceros's horns (p.67).

By Act II, Jean is busy rationalizing the irrational. There is a hollow ring to his justification of Bœuf's metamorphosis: 'Puisque ça lui fait plaisir de devenir rhinocéros ... Il n'y a rien d'extraordinaire à cela ... Je vous dis que ce n'est pas si mal que ça! Après tout, les rhinocéros sont des créatures comme nous' (p.158). His 'après tout', like the many stratagems of debate employed by Dudard ('dans le fond', 'tout de même', 'de toute façon', 'd'ailleurs', etc.[2]), is meant to shore up the none too solid edifice of his logic. Ultimately, his reasoning in favour of joining the rhinoceroses combines the hackneyed call for a return to nature with the rhetorical question 'why not?', to which there is really no answer: 'Pourquoi ne pas être un rhinocéros? J'aime les changements' (p.162). Ionesco shows us that, for all the façade of reason, Jean's — and everyone else's — reactions are totally irrational.

Botard, who is as much a rhinoceros of the left as Jean is one of the right, shares many of his characteristics. The empty-headedness of this 'fighter against ignorance' (p.99) is matched by his arrogance: 'Je ne crois que ce que je vois, de mes propres yeux ... j'aime la chose précise, scientifiquement prouvée, je suis un esprit méthodique, exact' (p.94). The word 'proof' features frequently in his vocabulary (as it does in Jean's), yet none of what he says carries any proof whatever. His assertions belong to the wildest fanaticism and prejudice. He, too, rejects the irrational — in Bérenger, for instance, (p.103) — except when he can dismiss it as madness. Just as Jean has put Bérenger's anguish down to a nervous disorder, 'la neurasthénie alcoolique' (p.43), Botard defines the rhinoceros craze as a 'psychose collective' (p.106),[3] a similarly erudite term. Botard is certainly surprised to see Bœuf changed into a rhinoceros, but not for long. In a rational world, every event must have a cause, there-

[2] These phrases are noted by Vernois who says of them: 'Elles caractérisent les justifications médiocres de Dudard qui accepte l'inévitable en tâchant de se donner bonne conscience' (*28*, p.243).

[3] The term also used elsewhere by Ionesco to define ideological hysteria (*15*, p.175).

fore 'il y a quelque chose là-dessous' (p.115). Flying in the face
of 'scientific proof', he has soon explained it away to his own
satisfaction as a capitalist plot, the details of which he keeps to
himself: 'Je comprends tout...' (p.119); 'Je vous l'expliquerai...
un jour... Je connais le pourquoi des choses, les dessous de
l'histoire...' (p.128). His ideology may be ruffled, but his faith
in the principle of cause and effect stays secure. Botard's
rationality is a hollow slogan, riddled with such contradictions
as: 'Ce n'est pas parce que je méprise les religions qu'on peut
dire que je ne les estime pas' (p.98).

This survey of the characters' pretence of logic would not be
complete without Bérenger, who, scarcely less than his fellows,
would like to be able to find comfort in reason. However, while
they cling to it at all costs and follow it wherever it leads them,
Bérenger, whose view of life as 'anormale' makes him more dis-
posed to recognize the absurd, becomes increasingly dis-
illusioned as rationality proves itself less and less adequate to
describe the world. From the outset, the Logician sets the tone
of the play with his pronouncement, 'La peur est irrationnelle.
La raison doit la vaincre' (p.27). But Bérenger's malaise is
precisely due to fear, to his sense of the unknown, which he can
only evoke as something vague and incomprehensible: 'Je ne sais
pas trop. Des angoisses difficiles à définir' (p.42).

He himself plays as large a part in the irrelevant discussions of
Acts I and II as anyone else. His society demands faith in
reason, and, up to a point, he conforms. For instance, in his
desire to be reconciled with Jean, he is no more rigorous in his
logic than the equivocating Dudard: 'Je tiens donc à vous dire,
mon cher Jean, que, chacun à sa façon, nous avions raison tous
les deux. Maintenant, c'est prouvé' (p.141). No more convincing
is his diagnosis of Jean's sickness as 'un excès de santé' (p.143),
with its alarming fascist overtones. In more intellectual matters,
he is hardly more successful. As it happens, he is right when he
corrects Jean's showy, zoological data on rhinoceros horns
(p.70), and, although he confuses him with Zeno, he quotes
Galileo accurately (p.196). But he soon gets hopelessly muddled
on both counts, since it is a level on which he cannot possibly
compete.

Only after he has witnessed Jean's transformation — which he considers in rational terms: 'Et pourtant, il avait des arguments, il semblait avoir réfléchi à la question, mûri sa décision' (p.178) — and after his vain attempts to counter Dudard's specious arguments, does he begin to appreciate the irrational implications of the epidemic, and become aware of the futility of debate and its patina of logic. He cannot accept Dudard's calm detachment, for when you are emotionally involved in the irrational, objective reasoning becomes impossible (p.184). Unwisely, he has tried to vie with Dudard on rational grounds, despite their inability to define either his own feelings or the blind charge of the rhinoceros-like mind. Integrity, feeling and reason itself are trampled underfoot, so he finally surrenders: 'Alors là, je... refuse de penser!' (p.197). This is not to be confused with the mental vacuum enjoyed by the other characters. What he means is that he refuses to think along rational lines — you cannot reason with a rhinoceros.

Nevertheless, Bérenger does not find it easy to renounce reason in favour of intuition. For some time, he wavers between the irrationality of anger, addressing his invective to the rhinoceroses — 'Salauds!' (pp.199, 200) — and the strong lure of logic. He still wants to turn to the Logician, 'un intellectuel subtil, érudit' (p.199), but, of course, the dotty philosopher has been absorbed by the forces of insanity, marking the final collapse of logic. In addition, Bérenger still seeks reasons for the abdication of others, like Botard: 'C'est parce qu'ils sont de bonne foi, on peut les duper' (p.207); and Dudard: 'C'est par dépit amoureux qu'il a fait cela. C'était un timide!' (pp.218-19). Almost to the end, he longs for what he sees as the benefits of scholarship: 'Je deviendrai érudit' (p.225), he tells Daisy to impress her. Only very slowly, as he experiences firstly love and then despair, does he abandon rationality entirely and give way to the deeper impulses which form his resistance.

We should be careful to make a distinction between two types of irrationality: that of Bérenger's resistance, based on emotion and instinct, and that of a world which is dependent on reason, but which has gone out of control. It is a distinction which Ionesco has made clear: 'L'illogisme (cachant une autre logique)

des rêves est tout à fait différent de l'illogisme du mécanisme
déréglé, lequel ... n'est pas à proprement parler un illogisme
mais une logique poussée à l'extrême' (*22*, p.120). With the
exception of Bérenger, the characters of *Rhinocéros* do not
abandon their logic. They simply distort it to suit their ends —
or perhaps we should say that it distorts them. In our relative
world, the absolutism of logic is a seductive, but highly
dangerous system. It contains within it, according to Ionesco,
the seeds of madness — 'toutes les folies possibles' (*22*, p.121).
All rational systems which seek to give an appearance of order to
the mysterious, complex experience of life, force reality into a
mould which does not fit it, destroying our wonder as well as our
bewilderment, and robbing us of freedom. For Ionesco, they are
a deception: 'Plus un système est parfait ... logique, cohérent,
plus il est irréel, artificiel. Tous les systèmes sont donc fonda-
mentalement artificiels, éloignés de la réalité' (*15*, p.67).

Logic is, for Ionesco, the prototype of all systems, systems
which man builds in the hope of protecting himself from,
perhaps even of curing himself of, the absurd, but they are, at
best, an illusion, and, at worst, a tyranny. Yet all around us,
there is just such a system, protecting us like the walls of a prison
— the structure, or structures, of society.

6. Society and the Individual

It is not Ionesco's purpose to write social satire. If it were, his work might appear somewhat uninspired. The puppet-like caricatures, the gross, farcical effects, the fairly predictable targets, and so on, would place his drama alongside certain examples of the boulevard theatre he despises. What is more, it would suggest that he considered the world to be funny; in fact, he finds it both laughable and horrific: 'Le monde peut être comique et dérisoire, il peut aussi vous sembler tragique, en tout cas il n'est pas drôle' (*18*, p.327). The very conception he has of comedy — 'le comique est effrayant, tragique' (*22*, p.51) — should be enough to imply that there is more at stake than the ridiculing of human foibles and social habits.

Nevertheless, he does ridicule these things, but, rather than for any superficial, satirical motive, it forms part of his more universal intention. Man's dilemma, as we have seen, is to find himself existing in a mysterious world, thirsting after understanding, and meeting only silence. He is 'coupé de ses racines essentielles' (*22*, p.137), out of harmony with the world. As we saw with the more abstract and intellectual umbrella of logic, his habit is to construct for himself a more comfortable habitat, built on rational lines, an inner compartment padded out with society's logical forms. The analogy that comes to mind is of a family carrying on as usual in a fall-out bunker, while the earth outside has been ravaged by atomic warfare. Of course, we do not blame the family for seeking refuge, any more than we condemn Bérenger, sheltering from danger at the end of *Rhinocéros*. What Ionesco finds unacceptable is that, within our bunker, we close our minds to the real problem outside the walls. Consequently, we squabble and fret about the solvable problems, the political and social problems which divide us, instead of uniting as individuals to face the insoluble problem of our common existence: 'Une fraternité fondée sur la métaphysique est plus sûre qu'une fraternité ou une camaraderie fondée sur la politique' (*18*, p.325).

Self-deception is an ineffectual defence. One of Dudard's countless platitudes, 'Et puis si on se faisait des soucis pour tout ce qui se passe, on ne pourrait plus vivre' (p.184), expresses the indifference to the absurd by which he and his fellow men manage to live, and which turns the toughness of their skins into armour-plating. The walls of our social sanctuary — authority, justice, convention, order — are not proof against the absurd. When it seeps through, as it is bound to do, we are suddenly brought face to face with the irrational (e.g. the appearance of a rhinoceros), for which we are not prepared. We try to cope by appealing to our familiar, logical structures (e.g. 'Nous devrions protester auprès des autorités municipales!' p.34), but our ways of thinking are not compatible with the problem, and they break down. The ensuing madness then needs to be tidied up and assimilated by reason ('Alors, assimilez la chose et dépassez-la' p.186), so that order can be restored. Thus society comes to justify and incorporate the antisocial (e.g. human beings changing into rhinoceroses) to form a new order. As Dudard cheerfully says, 'Peut-on savoir où s'arrête le normal, où commence l'anormal?' (p.195).

The discrediting of a society organized on rational and conformist lines runs throughout Ionesco's theatre. He often presents a social setting which is recognizably middle-class (parodying the 'théâtre de boulevard') and introduces into it a world of contradiction and madness. Many of his earlier plays open on a petty-bourgeois interior which clashes with the illogical events which occur within it. In *Rhinocéros*, the opening scene has expanded into the street (though still the closed world of a square), but the general atmosphere is similar, emphasized by the café and the shop-front. This ordinary scene, depicting an orderly society, is a deliberately incongruous setting for a charging rhinoceros.

The closed world of society depends upon the maintenance of order — logic incarnate in the shape of authority and justice. The text of the play contains a number of references to 'the authorities', faceless bureaucrats whose slightly menacing presence is felt but not seen. They are the impersonal 'on' of Jean's 'On ne devrait pas le permettre!' (p.34), and of Bérenger's 'On devrait les parquer dans de vastes enclos, leur imposer des résidences surveillées' (p.210). They are the means by which the individual townspeople can divest themselves of responsibility, leaving their own consciences clear. Thus it is with these self-styled protectors of public order in mind that Jean says they should complain to the council (p.34). Botard, too, puts his faith in a similar group of worthies (though they may well be the opposition) when he affirms: 'Je vais prendre contact avec les autorités compétentes' (p.133). Bérenger also relies on the authorities, only to find they have, like all successful administrations, sensed the changing wind and tacked accordingly: 'Les autorités sont passées de leur côté' (p.232). As administrators of the new conformism, with control of the information services, it is they, above all, who confirm the totalitarian implications of the play.

It comes as no surprise that Ionesco hates authority, based as it is on the will to power and the control of the many by the few. He writes: 'Toute autorité est arbitraire, même si cet arbitraire est appuyé par une foi ou bien une idéologie facile à démystifier' (*15*, p.25). He also declares: 'Je préfère le désordre à la tyrannie' (*15*, p.111).

The authorities in *Rhinocéros* seem slow to look after the wellbeing of the populace — not surprisingly, perhaps, since they represent the conformism and indifference which bring the mass transformation about. Thus, M. Papillon's unseen board of directors, in favour of whom he, too, disclaims responsibility — 'Ce n'est pas à moi de décider' (p.127) — has failed to see about renewing his rotting staircase (p.116).[4] In similar vein, Botard turns to anonymous committees — his 'comité d'action' (p.120) and his 'délégation' (p.121). Though they stand in opposition to the reigning conformism, they are authority in embryo, the administration of the future, which (after the revolution, no doubt) will impose its own brand of conformism.

Finally, among the forces of order, come the firemen. Though

[4] Note that eventually the new stairs will be made, not of cement, as Papillon wanted, but of wood, a suitably natural substance (p.188).

they play a fairly insignificant part in *Rhinocéros*, they are
something of an Ionesco trademark, appearing or being
mentioned in a large number of his plays. It appears that
firemen, as officials of the state, are part of Romanian folklore.
Be that as it may, Ionesco's obsession with them no doubt stems
from their position as powerful guardians of social order, organized along military lines, complete with uniform — the instru-
ment of depersonalization *par excellence*. In Act II, we only see
a head in its imposing helmet, and the precision of the stage
direction is worthy of note: 'On voit apparaître le casque d'un
Pompier, puis le Pompier' (p.131). In Act III, though we do not
see them at all, the description of the 'régiment' swarming from
the ruins of its 'caserne' adds considerably to the impression of
terror provoked by what seems increasingly like a military take-
over:

> BERENGER: Tous les pompiers, tout un régiment de rhino-
> céros, tambours en tête.
> DAISY: Ils se déversent sur les boulevards! (p.213)

What authority guarantees above all is justice. Given that a
system of justice is the backbone of organized society, Ionesco
predictably shows scant respect for the rule of law, as when he
writes: 'Je sais que toute justice est injuste' (*15*, p.25). When it is
equated with logic in Act I — 'Car la justice, c'est la logique';
'La justice, c'est encore une facette de la logique' (p.57) — we
are prepared for the bad light in which it is shown in the rest of
the play. The office represented in Act II is that of a business
specializing in legal publications, probably like the one in which
Ionesco himself worked for five years after the war. There is
little evidence of either justice or logic in the discussion which
takes place there, especially since it is dominated by Botard's
contradictions and prejudices. Although they play secondary
roles here, the two senior men of law, M. Papillon and Dudard,
are scarcely any more impressive, with, for example, their incon-
sequential reactions to the information that the rhinoceros
below is their colleague, Bœuf:

M. PAPILLON: Par exemple! Cette fois, je le mets à la porte
pour de bon!
DUDARD: Est-il assuré? (p.119)

Dudard's matter-of-fact question to his boss, after Mme Bœuf
has leaped on to her husband's armoured back, prepares us for
his legalistic impartiality in the final act: 'Vous avez déjà fait de
l'équitation?' (p.124). As a successful graduate of law, Dudard,
when he comes to the fore in Act III, shows justice proving
whatever the brief — or ideology — requires. It clearly has
nothing to do with good and evil.

Besides these unflattering insights into the judicial mind, some
more practical aspects of law and order are discernible. Dudard,
for instance, is working on 'la loi sur la répression anti-
alcoolique' (p.107), which recalls Jean's censure of Bérenger's
drinking. In Act III, when Bérenger is totally besieged by the
rhinoceroses, he refers to two petty regulations which strike us
as highly incongruous in the circumstances. Firstly, he cannot
disconnect the telephone, because 'Les P.T.T. ne permettent
pas' (p.231); secondly, his rhinoceros neighbours should not
threaten to bring the ceiling down, because: 'Défendu de faire
du bruit' (p.233). As he himself predicted, 'la loi morale' has
been replaced by 'la loi de la jungle' (p.159). The rational form
of law has proved ill-equipped to cope with the more primitive
forces of the absurd.

In addition to its codified law, society relies for its stability on
a set of conventions, and it is in his mockery of these supremely
conformist principles that Ionesco is at his most satirical. Even
here, however, it is not satire for its own sake. Conventions of
tidiness, politeness, punctuality, routine, etc. are by definition
the enemies of spontaneity, originality and individual freedom,
and his treatment of them is intimately associated with the major
themes of his play.

For Jean, it would appear that tidiness is next to godliness.
Always prepared, he produces from his unbulging pockets an
amazing assortment of items to correct the 'disorder' of
Bérenger's appearance. In Jean's mind, the world is as orderly
as a well-fitting suit and polished shoes, and, when this idea is

pushed to the extreme, nothing can be tidier than the dark-green uniform of a rhinoceros. The desire for orderliness is shared by all, as we see in the gathering together of La Ménagère's provisions — 'Remettez-les méthodiquement' (p.30) — and in the clearing up of broken glasses, which occupies Le Patron far more than a passing rhinoceros (pp.63-65).

Apart from Bérenger's clothes, his mind, too, must conform to a model of neatness: Jean demands of him sobriety (as do Dudard and Daisy) and culture. It may not be immediately obvious how the idea of culture fits into Jean's conventional outlook. On the face of it, his advice appears sound: visit the museums, read the literary reviews ('books' might have been better), go to lectures, see an Ionesco play. But Jean has clearly not gained much from Ionesco himself. No wonder, since 'culture' for him means being up to date and in the fashion — another sign of his conformism. It involves no deeply spiritual experience: 'En quatre semaines, vous êtes un homme cultivé' (p.54).

One of Ionesco's favourite targets among social conventions is the façade of politeness. In *Les Chaises*, for instance, the old couple talk to their invisible guests with a disarming mixture of courteousness and rudeness, all in the same tone, as if these were scarcely distinguishable from each other. In *Rhinocéros*, Ionesco exaggerates and highlights the convention, displaying its hollowness. It is most noticeable in the Vieux Monsieur's gallant behaviour to La Ménagère. This is mostly made up of platitudes, is noted as a national trait — 'Ah! la politesse française!' (p.31) — and is the prelude to a more than friendly interest in her welfare. A little later, the same Gentleman interrupts Bérenger twice to say 'N'interrompez pas' (p.84), and he continues to interrupt the Logician. Similarly, at the end of Act II, tableau I, Bérenger and Dudard become involved in a long exchange of 'Après vous', and end up by climbing out on to the ladder together (p.135). It is a well-tried, music-hall gag which never fails. Politeness receives its crowning accolade in Act III, when Dudard insists that Bérenger be more polite to the rhinoceroses. It would seem that the latter's distraught horror at what is happening 'n'est pas une raison pour être grossier' (p.200). The world is disintegrating into madness, but all Dudard can think of is good manners and the semblance of order they preserve.

Our society is obsessed by time. It marks our passage to old age and death, yet we worship it as a fetish. For Ionesco, it is time above all which makes life intolerable: 'Dès que nous sommes dans la dimension ou dans la durée, c'est l'enfer' (*22*, p.39). The society of *Rhinocéros* appears to believe that routine and punctuality are the road to Utopia: 'je fais tous les jours mes huit heures de bureau, moi aussi, je n'ai que vingt et un jours de congé par an...' (p.20). Routine is the primary artifice devised by man for casting a camouflage of order over the absurd. It is not surprising, therefore, that Bérenger arrives late for his appointment with Jean, as well as at the office, where the 'feuille de présence' is much in evidence. This world, which he cannot get used to, and where he senses the absurd, is ill-defined by the office clock. Death, after all, does not clock in and out. Jean, on the other hand, 'n'[a] pas de temps à perdre' (p.15). His life is governed by a 'programme' (p.57) and he charges off in Act I because he is 'wasting his time' talking to Bérenger (p.74). The sober Dudard, too, is controlled by routine, since he 'never has a drink before lunch' (p.180), while M. Papillon, quite impervious to the threat of the rhinoceroses, worries incessantly about the time lost in the office and which will have to be made up (pp.106, 126, 130, 132).

As the incarnation of conformism, therefore, society, in Ionesco, is an enlargement of the petty-bourgeois mind — 'le petit bourgeois étant l'homme des idées reçues, des slogans, le conformiste de partout' (*13*, p.253). But the problem goes deeper. Society, as an artificial panoply of order, and like those other abstractions, nation and race, is an example of what Ionesco calls 'ce goût de la collectivité' and 'cette tentative actuelle de dépersonnalisation' (*15*, p.166). The collectivity is only human if it is a society of individuals. But society tends to engulf the individual, particularly in the urban setting so characteristic of modern life. Looking back on his life, Ionesco contrasts the luminous, free existence he enjoyed as a small child in the village of La Chapelle-Anthenaise, with his later life in Paris and Bucharest:

> Là, tout était plus petit, plus à l'échelle humaine. Le village était un cosmos, à la fois le nid et l'espace, la solitude nécessaire et la communauté. Ce n'était pas un monde limité, c'était un monde complet. Tout le monde, toutes choses avaient un visage... Tout était personnalisé, concret. (*22*, p.17)

Scale obviously plays a large part in this nostalgic memory.[5] However, external factors alone do not account for what he feels is wrong with modern society. What matters is its dehumanized quality, the attitude of mind which reduces the human being to a function, and allows the social unit to usurp the status of the individual. The essential problem which this creates is that of solitude, an ambiguous and central theme in Ionesco's theatre.

Beneath the impersonal cloak of bureaucracy, and in the bustle of the crowd, the individual loses his identity. While he is cut off from his inner self in this way, he is also cut off from others for the same reason. (This is why Bérenger says: 'La solitude me pèse. La société aussi' (p.45).) Isolated and lonely, he and his fellows suffer 'la solitude en commun' (*22*, p.126). Ionesco makes an important distinction between this form of solitude, which is isolation and estrangement, and the more constructive solitude which individuals need for their spiritual lives and for meditation — even if this means contemplation of the absurd: 'La solitude n'est pas l'isolement, elle n'est pas une barrière me séparant du monde, elle est un bouclier, une cuirasse, qui peut défendre ma liberté' (*14*, p.179). Solitude, as opposed to isolation, is therefore of vital importance to man, and the key to his unhappiness in society is that he is lonely but never truly alone. The characters in Ionesco's plays fill their silence with chatter because they are afraid of solitude, but in so doing, they deprive themselves of any spiritual existence. They are isolated within the crowd, and they are separated also from their inner, metaphysical selves, their 'troisième dimension' (*14*, p.56). The individual, in so far as he is defined by his inner life, is therefore destroyed by society, yet it is only at an individual level that true communication and true companionship can

[5] Contrast Dudard's 'Je préfère la grande famille universelle à la petite' (p.216).

exist. Without this, individuality becomes egoism, self-importance, indifference to others and to the world. It is only in real communication between individuals, which we find in Ionesco in the themes of friendship and love, that man can rediscover a basis for society with a human face.

Once again, the point is clearly illustrated by the differing attitudes of Jean and Bérenger. For all his apparent solicitude, Jean shows little fellow-feeling, since he is only trying to make Bérenger more like himself. His statement, 'J'ai honte d'être votre ami' (p.19), discloses the shallowness of his sympathy. His frequent use of phrases like 'mon pauvre ami' (p.36) and 'mon cher ami' (p.42) rings hollow, the emptiness of the clichés echoing the absence of sentiment. If Bérenger is too indulgent towards his overbearing companion, it is primarily because of his need for friendship: 'Vous savez à quel point je vous estime' (p.39), he insists. He is deeply upset by their quarrel — 'J'ai le cœur trop gros' (p.88) — accepts all the blame, and goes to great lengths to repair their relationship. Their contrasting attitudes to others is also revealing. Bérenger has been to a party given by 'notre ami Auguste'; he could not refuse, he says, because 'Cela n'aurait pas été gentil' (p.21). In similar circumstances, Jean is less concerned about the feelings of others; he cannot go out with Bérenger because he is meeting other friends. He will keep his appointment, not out of 'gentillesse', but as a point of honour: 'J'ai promis d'y aller. Je tiens mes promesses' (p.58). In Act II, as his position becomes more extreme, he declares openly his lack of human warmth: 'L'amitié n'existe pas. Je ne crois pas en votre amitié' (p.151). There is nothing new about his misanthropy: it is a natural extension of the coldness and egoism he has already displayed. By shielding himself from the emotional involvement required for deeper human contact, he ends by renouncing human society itself: 'A vrai dire, je ne déteste pas les hommes, il me sont indifférents, ou bien ils me dégoûtent' (p.152).

The love affair between Bérenger and Daisy takes this question a stage further. As the archetypal couple seeking to 'régénérer l'humanité' (p.236) on the basis of love, they represent 'l'humanité divisée et qui essaie de se réunir, de

s'unifier' (*22*, p.83). Bérenger's repeated protestations of love
express partly his wonderment, and partly his need for love to
provide an outlet for his feelings: 'Ah! Daisy, je croyais que je
n'allais plus jamais pouvoir devenir amoureux d'une femme'
(p.220). In stifling his passion — his capacity for passion —
society has stifled his life as an individual, but in this new union
of souls, he feels liberated. His headache, representing his fears
for his moral existence, is cured, and, as visual confirmation,
Daisy takes off his bandage: 'Tu me libères de mes complexes ...
Avec toi, je n'aurai plus d'angoisses' (p.224). In many of
Ionesco's plays, similar claims are made for love as a release
from anguish. On each occasion, however, it fails: 'L'amour est
notre atmosphère vitale, notre pain quotidien. Hélas! l'atmosphère est viciée, le pain empoisonné' (*14*, p.137). So it is with
Daisy and Bérenger. Daisy lacks the courage to face the spiritual
challenge of her new-found individuality because it gives her
back her solitude, as well as the emotional life, the guilt and the
metaphysical anguish that come with it. These are symbolized by
the headache and the bandage, which now pass to her (p.234).
Her fears and her need to escape from them into conformity
overcome her love. The last hope for human society has dis-
appeared, for, as she observes, 'La vie en commun n'est plus
possible' (p.242), a fact graphically illustrated by Bérenger's
desperate isolation in the final scene.

In that final scene, Bérenger can only contemplate his own
image in the mirror. Robbed of the spiritual bond which
promised him new life as an individual, he now suffers loneliness
and isolation, the destructive face of solitude. In vain, he looks
around himself for companionship which would give meaning to
his individuality, but always he returns to his own image. Devoid
of meaning, his individuality threatens to disintegrate: 'Est-ce
que je me comprends?... A quoi je ressemble alors?' (p.244),
and he can no longer recognize whether photographs are of himself or of others. His individuality begins to horrify him and he
longs to renounce it, to merge into the crowd of rhinoceroses.
However, a deeper instinct — further evidence of his spiritual
identity — makes him cling to this precious sign of his humanity,
however ugly and painful it proves to be, and he cannot change.

At the last moment, he rediscovers, in place of barren isolation, a kind of strength in solitude, reminiscent of the image used by Ionesco to define it and which I quoted a little earlier: 'un bouclier, une cuirasse, qui peut défendre ma liberté'.

7. The Language of Drama

Je ne fais pas de littérature. Je fais une chose tout à fait différente; je fais du théâtre. Je veux dire que mon texte n'est pas seulement un dialogue mais il est aussi 'indications scéniques'. (*13*, p.289)

Ionesco has directed some fairly sharp criticisms at producers who have used his plays as a pretext for their own flights of fancy. The one quoted above relates to an early American production of *Rhinocéros* which had made all sorts of ill-advised additions to the text. It is important to remember that while literature is made only of words, drama is written for performance and speaks to the eyes as well as the ears of the spectator. Ionesco is in the forefront of theatrical developments in the twentieth century, not least because of his extensive use of the total language of drama: set, props, sound, lighting, costume, gesture, rhythm, as well as the spoken text. He is a highly inventive dramatist and it goes without saying that no-one can fully appreciate an Ionesco play without seeing it well performed in the theatre. However, it is inevitable that many students of his works are obliged to make do with the printed text of a play. Nevertheless, all is not lost, as long as the reader, who must be producer, actor and spectator all at once, takes care to *visualize* as well as *hear* the text, remaining alert to all the stage directions and reading with the imagination.

Ionesco is a fierce opponent of the 'théâtre de boulevard' which still fills theatres throughout the western world — naturalistic or 'realist' drama, which glorifies mediocrity, claiming to imitate life but only touching the surface of reality, and which is, in Ionesco's words, 'sans problèmes, sans questions... Il n'inquiète pas, il ne rassure pas' (*18*, pp.326-27). His own theatre, on the other hand, 'met en question la totalité du destin de l'homme' (*18*, p.326), and the reality it seeks embraces the subconscious, the realm of our obsessions, desires and fears. For this, the traditional techniques of drama needed to be greatly expanded, and the total resources of the stage exploited.

In no way does it belittle Ionesco's originality to draw attention to some of the formative influences which have helped create his outstanding theatrical talent. It is beyond the scope of a short study such as this to undertake a full analysis of this complex subject, but I think it is necessary very briefly to mention the two main influences on his conception of theatre: Alfred Jarry and Antonin Artaud.

Jarry's *Ubu Roi* set out to shock Parisian audiences in 1896 with its notorious, opening, six-letter word and its disgusting, cruel and tyrannical figure of Ubu. He stood for 'tout le grotesque qu'il y ait au monde', the embodiment of the human condition. Ionesco sees him as an archetype which 'incarne la valeur et la vérité du mythe' and he acknowledges his debt to Jarry in making monsters of his own characters in *Rhinocéros* (*22*, p.188). Of particular interest to us are the indications which Jarry gave about the staging of *Ubu Roi*. He insisted on the 'guignol', or Punch and Judy, aspects of the play, by the use of masks, of horses' heads made of cardboard hung around the actors' necks, of settings indicated by placards (more suggestive than décor), of costumes which avoided historical accuracy — all adding to the impersonal effect and stressing the mythical and eternal quality of the idea.

Artaud is mainly remembered for his theoretical writings on the theatre, collected under the title *Le Théâtre et son double* (1938). Greatly influenced by the mystical and ritual drama of the Orient, he saw theatre as playing a metaphysical, almost religious role in people's lives, shocking them out of their preconceptions and revealing the hidden source of their fears and desires. He conceived of theatre as a total and evocative use of space — 'la poésie dans l'espace' — in which costume, set, lighting, sound, mime, etc. would all play their part. A written text was not essential, but words might be used for their sound quality, as incantation, rather than for their sense. It matters little that Artaud had only limited success in translating his ideas to the stage, and that Ionesco expresses some misgivings about

certain aspects of Artaud's approach. (Needless to say, the ideological type of campaign does not appeal to him.) The conception of theatre as 'poetry in space' has been fully assimilated
by Ionesco, who has developed it in his own way.

Ionesco has explained that he used to dislike the theatre. In his
younger days, he hardly ever went to see plays because they
mostly bored and embarrassed him. However, one spectacle,
that of a Punch and Judy show, did affect him deeply. He
watched it for hours, not laughing but spell-bound:

> Le spectacle du guignol me tenait là, comme stupéfait, par
> la vision de ces poupées qui parlaient, qui bougeaient, se
> matraquaient. C'était le spectacle même du monde, qui,
> insolite, invraisemblable, mais plus vrai que le vrai, se
> présentait à moi sous une forme infiniment simplifiée et
> caricaturale, comme pour en souligner la grotesque et
> brutale vérité. (*13*, p.53)

The show struck him by its quality as myth, its embodiment of
eternal and universal truth. It made no pretence of realism in the
narrow sense implied by our everyday reality. The visions of our
dreams and imagination reveal a deeper reality, with a metaphysical dimension, in which man's condition is brought into
question. By the expression of these visions, Ionesco's drama
seeks to rediscover the universality of myth in the theatre,
bringing together his own obsessions and those of humanity in
general: 'J'exprime ma solitude et je rejoins toutes les solitudes;
ma joie d'exister ou mon étonnement d'être sont ceux de tout le
monde' (*13*, p.87). It remains for theatre to give its own physical
form of expression to this inner world — 'matérialiser des
angoisses', 'concrétiser les symboles' (*13*, p.63) — going beyond
the power of words to communicate 'l'insoutenable'. It is
necessary, therefore, for theatre to enlist all its resources to
break out of the strait-jacket of realism and psychological
subtlety. In Ionesco's view, the way ahead lies in extreme exag-
geration:

> Le grossissement des effets... Non pas cacher les ficelles,

mais les rendre plus visibles encore... Aller à fond dans le
grotesque, la caricature... la charge parodique extrême...
Un comique dur, sans finesse, excessif... Pousser tout au
paroxysme, là où sont les sources du tragique. (*13*, pp.59-
60)

It is against the background of these ideas that we can start to
appreciate Ionesco's intentions and achievements in *Rhinocéros*.
The use of the frozen 'tableau vivant' at the opening of the first
two acts (see p.92) is a device which stems directly from the
puppet-theatre. By showing the characters as marionettes which
suddenly leap into life, like a mechanism that has been switched
on, the dramatist stresses the mythical quality of his work. We
are about to witness a caricature of life, a portrayal of universal,
not particular, truth. Within the theatre, according to Ionesco,
anything can be made to happen — it is a magical universe free
of the ordinary laws of nature. When Jean is transformed into a
rhinoceros, we do not need to ask whether such a thing is
possible — in the theatre, seeing is believing. We should therefore be careful how we judge an Ionesco play. Despite apparent
similarities with 'realistic' drama, it establishes, in fact, a quite
different set of criteria. For example, the traditional features of
dialogue and character are both present, but neither performs a
conventional function.

The spoken text of *Rhinocéros*, as we have seen, is largely
composed of platitudes and slogans, none of them intrinsically
interesting for its conceptual content, and all of them, by
definition, unoriginal. This prompts two questions: firstly, how
does the playwright keep his audience's attention, and secondly,
what is his purpose? The first question has been neatly
formulated by Richard Coe:

Ionesco's problem is that somehow the phrase whose very
essence is meaningless insignificance should become
significant without thereby becoming meaningful. It must
visibly destroy itself, reveal its own absurdity. Thus
Ionesco's platitudes are more than simple commonplaces;
they are commonplaces which *compel the attention*. (*24*,
p.48)

They compel our attention by virtue of their sheer abundance, their stark contradictions, their complacent empty-headedness, their stunning irrelevance, and, of course, their humour. We cannot expect such words directly to communicate a message, or to reveal character, or to be the driving force of a plot. Language has become a dramatic object; its true meaning lies, not in what it says, but in what it is. The text itself is being used by Ionesco as a symbol of the inner vacuum.

Character, too, can be interpreted in a similar way. Like the language they speak, the characters are the barest stereotypes, descendants of Punch and Judy rather than of M. and Mme Jourdain. They are little more than puppets, representing, not a particular society, but the condition of mankind. It is central to Ionesco's purpose to give a metaphysical, rather than social, dimension to psychology: it is not man-in-society but man-in-the-world that he finds both interesting and derisory. In *Rhinocéros*, the characters are not even clearly distinguishable from one another — appropriately, since their conformity leads them all to the same end. We can discern Jean's dictatorial conservatism, Botard's militant trade-unionism, Dudard's non-committal (or liberal?) legalism — each with a smattering of suitable vocabulary. But there is at the same time a considerable overlap between all three of them, while even the coquettish Daisy, who, until the end, conserves a trace of individuality, comes to sound like Dudard and Jean as she disappears into the crowd.

These are two-dimensional characters, lacking psychological depth. They are objects of the drama with a symbolic function like that of language or the elements of the set. Although each can be said to represent some aspect of society, their significance derives, not from each of them singly, but from their coherence as a group. Considered collectively, they represent the psychology of the crowd and 'le processus de la transformation collective' (*22*, p.69). Like the rhinoceros heads they become, they give material form to the nightmarish image of proliferation which was the dramatist's starting point, for it must be stressed that the horror provoked by the play arises not only from the presence of the rhinoceroses, but from the accelerating rhythm with which they come into being, closing the net around Bérenger.

Bérenger, of course, stands out as an exception. It was with *Tueur sans gages* (first performed 1959 — the same year that *Rhinocéros* opened in Düsseldorf) that Ionesco first introduced this figure of the dissenting individual into his plays. It would be misleading to consider him as 'l'homme raisonnable' — it is the others who are 'reasonable', whereas Bérenger's strength is founded of his appreciation of the irrational. He has been described as the 'Français moyen' (*28*, p.21), yet this, too, seems to belie his essential individuality, his role as the one out of step in *Rhinocéros*. It must be emphasized, however, that, in some respects, he is tarred with the same brush as his companions: he, too, can contradict himself; he, too, is steeped in platitude (though to a lesser extent); he, too, is prepared to conform (though his motive is friendship rather more than a belief in conformism). No doubt he represents what Ionesco has termed 'la vérité contradictoire de l'homme' (*15*, p.205): the individual is unique, defined by his difference, yet he is also the same as everyone else — a product of society, sharing the human condition with the rest of us. Bérenger, too, therefore, can be seen as a stereotype: the individual within the group, who clings to his individuality (his freedom, his inner life) as the only acceptable defence against 'l'insolite'.

Even as a representative of man's individuality, Bérenger is not a fully rounded character. Yet this is not a weakness on Ionesco's part. Bérenger's greater psychological depth is significant only when considered in relation to the shallowness of the other characters. It is by virtue of them that he is thrown into relief. The essential conflict in *Rhinocéros* is not between personalities, but between human and non-human values, between individuality and the conformist mass. The characters, as Vernois rightly defines them, are 'tout juste des pions sur un échiquier où la collectivité et l'individu s'affrontent' (*28*, p.120).

Much of the psychological content of Ionesco's plays is to be found outside the characters, in the material features of the set, props, costumes and stage directions. These are nearly always described in great detail, indicating to producer, technicians and actors precisely what is required in the matter of staging. (There is nothing dogmatic in this, and the author often adjusts his ideas in the light of rehearsals.) Nothing is left to chance because, for Ionesco, the physical aspects of the drama are the materialization of the inner world. Thus the contrasting costumes of Jean and Bérenger symbolize their different attitudes towards human existence. Jean's smartness, signifying his complacency, and Bérenger's untidiness, signifying his malaise, represent, not just their social outlook, but also their metaphysical awareness. When, in Act II, Jean strips off his pyjamas to expose his green skin, he is abandoning the last vestiges of human individuality. The clothes lie strewn about the room as a reminder of the disaster. Similarly, the head-bandage worn by Bérenger in Act III is a visual sign of his headache, the same headache as those which Jean (p.143) and Daisy (p.234) complain of. Each in turn, when faced with the choice of following the crowd or upholding his uniqueness, feels the full weight of individual responsibility pressing down on him. The headache and the bandage, therefore, represent in physical form the presence of man's sense of guilt and responsibility and the anguish which stems from it. It is a master-stroke on Ionesco's part to convert Jean's headache into a monstrous horn jutting from his forehead. Thus the individual's sense of responsibility is transformed into the guilt-free morality of the herd. Consequently, Bérenger's bandage, which briefly passes to Daisy, implies both treatment for his personal anguish and an attempt to suppress the temptation of the collective lie. It is characteristic of Ionesco to use a simple stage prop such as this to express and suggest far more than dialogue could do.

Throughout Ionesco's theatre, objects play a large and significant part. As in *Le Nouveau Locataire*, where furniture gradually fills the stage until it imprisons the new tenant in a few square feet of darkness, so the clutter of objects nearly always appears in a crescendo of proliferation. The animal heads which besiege Bérenger at the end of *Rhinocéros* perform much the same function as the furniture in the earlier play, the only difference being that Bérenger is an unwilling victim. The rhinoceroses, like most of the objects in Ionesco's work, represent man's abdication of his inner world, the renunciation of his essential humanity. It is particularly interesting that, when he fills the back wall with stylized rhinoceros heads, Ionesco indicates that 'Ces têtes devront être de plus en plus belles malgré leur monstruosité', and that their sounds become 'musicalisés' (p.219). Thus the monstrous can become alluring and seductive, just as ideologies can gain acceptance through familiarity and propaganda. They erode our judgement and change our way of seeing. Ionesco depicts this by contrasting the ugliness of the human portraits Bérenger hangs up (p.244) with the 'prettified' monsters — a further use of props to express an attitude of mind.

The set of Act I portrays a scene in a small provincial town. Church bells herald the rising of the curtain, but the religious world immediately gives way to that of commerce: the grocer's shop, marked 'EPICERIE' in large letters,[6] and the café, each with its upper storey, dominate the stage, with the church hidden some way behind them. The spiritual has literally been upstaged by the material, a fact reinforced by L'Epicière's opening remark with its tone of jealousy and mercenariness.

Outside the café, tables and chairs cover practically half the vacant stage. Like the meaningless talk which blocks out the metaphysical silence, objects are made to occupy the spiritual void. At first, everything in the scene expresses the town's sense of orderliness and peace; it is an image of the collective consciousness. Soon, however, we see chairs tipping over, La Ménagère's shopping basket spilling its contents over the floor, and the waitress's tray of glasses smashing to the ground, all of which creates a hilarious state of disorder. Their material world, like a barricade erected against the absurd, is under attack and is starting to crumble.

Act II opens on an office, crowded with desks and chairs, papers and books. It is a world of order and routine and, above all, of objects. This time it is the building itself which starts to collapse, as the dehumanized Bœuf brings the staircase down. In

---

[6] The grocer's trade has a very bad image in France where the term 'épicier' is used pejoratively to describe someone who is small-minded, self-seeking and mercenary.

the second tableau, Jean's apartment also finishes in ruins, though the damage is now inflicted from the inside. After the floor has been strewn with bedding and clothes, the scene finishes with the bathroom door pierced by a horn and on the point of collapse, and the wall giving way under Bérenger's weight.

The similarity of Bérenger's room to that of Jean is deliberate and significant: 'C'est la chambre de Bérenger, qui ressemble étonnamment à celle de Jean' (p.169). In this way, Ionesco takes into account the practical difficulties of staging, while stressing the superficial conformity of their lives. Even Bérenger's home, the final bastion of humanity, shows signs of crumbling: 'Du plâtre tombe du plafond. La maison s'ébranle violemment' (p.233). All around we hear of walls being flattened. Everywhere, the old order, with whatever illusory hope it offered to mankind, is rapidly collapsing, its apparent solidity having proved itself more of a trap than a defence.

All three tableaux of Acts II and III depict an upper storey, served by a staircase. This forms a precarious refuge above the street-level domain of the rhinoceroses, but it soon comes to resemble a prison. The humans are marooned in their office, and are forced to climb down among the animals, exposing themselves to contamination. The movements of the characters begin to illustrate their imprisonment. Jean paces his room 'comme une bête en cage' (p.152) and Bérenger, who is trapped there with him, has to recoil from every exit, finally resorting to desperate measures in order to escape. In Act III, before his final desertion, Dudard 'se met à tourner en rond' (p.217), recalling the caged movements of both M. Bœuf and Jean in the previous act. Later, both Bérenger and Daisy run from window to window, repeatedly meeting up face to face in the centre of the room (pp.220, 231, 232). These movements describe the narrowing confines of their freedom and help to express their terror as the hostile world closes in on them. We might add to this that the successive scenes of the play tend to create a growing sense of imprisonment. Having begun in the open air, the rhinoceros menace pursues Bérenger first to his place of work, then into his friend's flat, and finally traps him in his most intimate surroundings, his own home.

An important feature of the set for both Acts II and III is the window placed at the front of the stage, through which the characters look out on to the audience. Not only does this add to the impression of siege, it also shows the rhinoceroses coming from the direction of the auditorium — Ionesco's challenge to our own individuality.

Throughout the play, Ionesco makes extensive use of an unusual symbol, that of dust. An incongruous element of the opening set is 'un arbre poussiéreux' (p.13), giving the one living thing a rather drab appearance, as if everything were not well with society after all. Similarly, the set of Act II contains 'des rangées de livres et de dossiers poussiéreux' (p.92). Dust makes its presence felt more obviously early in Act I, when Bérenger brushes some from his jacket, causing Jean to turn his head away (p.19). Most significantly, it is an accompaniment to the rhinoceroses and signals their destructive presence. When the first one passes, it sends clouds of dust over the scene, making Jean sneeze and Bérenger blow his nose, exclaiming: 'Ça en fait de la poussière!' (p.26). When M. Bœuf brings the staircase down (p.113), and when an outside wall is heard to collapse (p.212), dust totally engulfs the characters. Their feeble reactions — 'La poussière va salir les assiettes'; 'Quel manque d'hygiène!' (pp.212-13) — are a reminder of the irrelevant values held dear by society and which are now brought into question.

This recurrent image of dust implies that the world is not as ordered and pure as the characters would like to believe. It suggests decay and an irrational presence which threatens the neat structures of society. It contrasts with the whiteness and unnatural clarity — 'lumière crue, murs très blancs' — of the street scene in Act I, where it may represent the presence of the absurd which until now has been ignored by all except Bérenger. It becomes a symptom of the rhinoceritis epidemic, a visual image of the spiritual sickness which has overtaken society, precisely because it has tried to sweep the absurd under the carpet.

This interesting symbol gives further meaning also to other

metaphorical elements in the play. For instance, Jean, who has
accused his friend of being 'dans les brumes épaisses de l'alcool'
(p.36), claims clarity of mind for himself — 'Moi, je ne suis pas
dans le brouillard... J'ai l'esprit clair' (p.69) — as if he himself
were immune from the haze of the irrational. Moreover, in Acts
II and III, when both Jean and Bérenger suffer from uncontrol-
lable coughs, this may be seen as an extension of the dust image,
a spontaneous reaction to the manifestation of the absurd. In
Jean's case, the symptom is absorbed into his being, and, like his
headache becoming a horn, so his voice grows more and more
husky until it turns into the roar of a rhinoceros.

Crucial to the effect of Ionesco's plays is their pace or rhythm.
This characteristic feature, difficult to describe but easily
detected in performance, is usually experienced as a giddying
acceleration, accompanied by a proliferation of objects (or
words), and creating the impression of a world spinning out of
control. *Rhinocéros* is no exception, as its race of monsters
increases inexorably, engulfing the human characters as it does
so. At the beginning, the stage is crowded with people, ten of
them in all. Gradually the rhinoceroses impose themselves, but
they remain invisible, no more than a sound effect and a cloud
of dust. However, once we have seen one actually take shape in
Jean's room, they become increasingly present, audibly and
visually. While the number of humans dwindles to one, the
beasts proliferate wildly, encircling the entire stage and pene-
trating even Bérenger's room.

Ionesco has described the movement of the play as 'une idée
simple, une progression également simple et une chute' (*13*,
p.286). In fact, this oversimplifies the intricacies of its structure.
It proceeds by alternating periods of relative calm with bursts of
acceleration. The tension rises to form a series of peaks, such as
when the rhinoceroses go past in Act I (accompanied by Jean's
mounting fury and a crescendo of sound); when, in Act II, M.
Bœuf's activities create panic in the office; or when an ever
wilder movement takes command of the action, as when Jean
goes on the rampage and Bérenger dashes this way and that,
gripped by terror and desperation. Act III returns us to a more
static atmosphere and develops the tension more slowly. We

may feel, I think, that here the drama moves a little too slowly and relies too heavily on the verbal text during the long debate between Bérenger and Dudard. In the Bérenger-Daisy scene, the pace quickens, thanks to greater movement and more rapid exchanges. It is also more varied, as the couple bicker, are reconciled, express their love, and quarrel again. The scene is punctuated by frenzied activity, as when they rush round the room and come to a halt in the middle, when he slaps her face and she weeps, or when he runs out after her and returns in despair. All these alternating ups and downs prepare the final catastrophe (the 'chute'). In the last scene, Bérenger's short phrases and his furious movements express his anger and despair. Yet, at the very last moment, it is as if he suddenly finds his feet on the slippery slope of disintegration, as despair is replaced by the dignity of resistance and his wild movements give way to a static tableau: the confrontation of the individual and the mass. It is an image of considerable dramatic power.

Powerful as it is, this final image is marked by ambiguity. It is possible to see Bérenger's last stand either as heroic, or, since it is surely a futile gesture, as derisory. Bérenger is not a hero in the traditional sense; he is naive and weak and lacks resolution. Does he come to realize what is right and defend it unflinchingly against all the odds? If so, he achieves greatness. Yet he wavers and longs to end his suffering by defecting to the enemy. Martin Esslin has written: 'Far from being a heroic last stand, Bérenger's defiance is farcical and tragicomic' (*31*, p.180). Certainly, if he only chooses to resist out of 'sour grapes', then greatness is merely thrust upon him.

In considering this question, it is as well to bear in mind Ionesco's own difficulty in the thirties in arguing against a fashionable, all-pervasive ideology: 'En effet, quand on pense seul contre les autres, contre tous, on ne peut pas avoir bonne conscience' (*18*, p.97). Only when he found support for his own views in France after 1938 was his flagging will strengthened: 'C'était ainsi qu'une bonne conscience retrouvée me permettait de ne pas succomber à la rhinocérite' (*18*, p.97). It is important, therefore, for him to show Bérenger's hesitancy, since it demonstrates the enormous power of the germ. We are presented with a Bérenger having all the inherent weakness of an ordinary individual, which makes his final show of courage all the more heroic.

Nevertheless, Ionesco is not content merely to leave us with an image of his hero's dignity. Immediately before his sudden resolution at the end, Bérenger pathetically attempts to imitate the herd's 'barrissements' (p.245). The ridiculous sounds he utters deliberately work against the sympathy we may feel for him. In effect, the scene produces that mixed response which characterizes Ionesco's view of the human condition: a mixture of pity and derision. If we are tempted to smile at him, it is with a grim smile which freezes on our lips. When he finally turns away from us to face the back wall, which is covered with rhinoceros heads, we are made to share his impossible dilemma, but we share his weakness as well as his heroism, his comedy as well as his tragedy. This conforms to what Ionesco sees as the essence of drama: 'Seul ce qui est insoutenable est profondément tragique, profondément comique, essentiellement théâtre' (*13*, p.52).

Rhinocéros depends for its total effect on this ambiguity. The play evolves from farce to a blend of black comedy and tragedy. In the second half, slapstick virtually disappears and verbal humour is far less pronounced; the comic element becomes more dependent on acceleration and mechanical movement. This is comedy of a more disturbing nature, one which lets the tragic show through.

Speaking of various productions of his play, Ionesco points out that it is possible to emphasize either of these ingredients, according to the extent to which props and accessories are used. For Jean's transformation scene, some original versions (e.g. in Germany and France) made full use of make-up — horn, green skin — whereas in others (e.g. in America and Romania), these devices were absent, allowing the character to change inwardly. He adds: 'Ce qui est curieux c'est que lorsqu'on n'emploie pas d'accessoires, la pièce devient plus noire, plus tragique; lorsqu'on les emploie, c'est comique, les gens rient' (*22*, p.103). Ionesco reserves most praise for Barrault's production which created 'une farce tragique' (*13*, p.289), and it would seem, judging by the published text, that the dramatist intended the comedy to be given its full value so that it may gradually reveal its tragic face. The derisory nature of life, as he sees it, will then be more accurately portrayed: 'Ce qu'il ne faut pas dans mes pièces, c'est lâcher l'insolite au profit du pathétique. Il faut éviter le pathétique; la dérision, l'ironie doivent l'emporter' (22, p.162). If this advice is followed for *Rhinocéros*, then Bérenger emerges, at the height of his heroism, as a representative of the human tragicomedy.

8. Conclusion

Students who come to Ionesco's work with little experience of modern drama frequently find it somewhat difficult to grasp. This is probably because in many cases it is far from easy to define what his plays are about. Inspired as they often are by dreams and the subconscious, their subject matter may seem elusive. Many of the early plays, especially, are the elaboration of an image, an experiment in dramatic form: 'une composition dramatique qui se veut plus nette, plus dépouillée, plus purement théâtrale' (*13*, p.87). Since its earliest productions, however, *Rhinocéros* has appealed to a wider audience, partly, no doubt, because its conception is more literary and its composition less pure. What is more, it has as its framework a fairly strong story-line, and one which is not too resistant to interpretation.

In part, despite being less theatrically pure, the play has achieved success, and promises to survive, by virtue of its power as drama, of its ability to find dramatic expression for human problems. By depicting in such a striking central image the monster in all of us, and by appealing to the Bérenger in all of us, it incarnates the blind stupidity of man as well as his individual solitude; and by placing these in confrontation, it creates a powerful myth, embodying a universal human dilemma.

But, undoubtedly, much of the play's appeal derives from the clarity of its theme and its relevance to the modern world. Unfortunately, the clarity that is claimed for it is often allowed to obscure the fact that, as I have tried to show in the preceding pages, it is a complex work combining many significant features and several layers of meaning. Its vitality as a work of art depends to a great extent on its ambiguities, on the tensions between comedy and tragedy and between the political and metaphysical themes.

Richard Coe has called *Rhinocéros* 'one of the most significant political plays of the twentieth century' (*24*, p.94) and, at
first glance, there seems little reason to dispute this judgement.
However deep its roots in the growth of fascism in the 1930s, its
applicability to contemporary issues makes it a play of much
wider relevance. Ionesco has been quick to extend its theme to
all totalitarian régimes: one immediately thinks of Hungary,
Czechoslovakia and Poland in recent years. Indeed, wherever
individual life and liberty are threatened by the clash of
ideologies, from Iran to Northern Ireland, *Rhinocéros* holds up
a derisive mirror to man's idolatry and fanaticism, to his cruelty
and tyranny.

Yet it is questionable whether such analogies account entirely
for the play's universal appeal. They may even, in fact, obscure
its essential meaning. Ionesco himself has surely come closest to
defining its wider — and deeper — significance:

> Je crois que si on a aimé cette pièce partout dans le monde,
> c'est parce que tous les pays maintenant, aussi bien à
> l'ouest qu'à l'est, sont plus ou moins collectivisés. Plus ou
> moins inconsciemment j'ai mis la main sur un problème
> terrible: la dépersonnalisation. Or dans toutes les sociétés
> modernes les individus collectivisés ont la nostalgie de la
> solitude, d'une vie personnelle. (*22*, p.128)

Despite its political theme, then, is *Rhinocéros* really a political
play? Does such a label not ignore the crucial role of Bérenger,
who resists the political tide? He offers no counter-ideology
except the values of human fraternity. He is a human, not a
political, being: he stands, not for an alternative political
solution, but against all political solutions. In fact, the play is
probably more accurately described as *anti*-political, since, as
P.-A. Touchard has observed, Bérenger's refusal to capitulate is
not 'un refus politique en présence d'une option actuelle, mais
un refus de la politique dans la mesure où elle tend à aliéner
l'homme' (*37*, p.13). Bérenger opts only for human values, those
which defend his spirit.

Although deeply interested in political issues, Ionesco holds the view that politics, instead of providing an administrative framework allowing for 'le libre épanouissement de la vie spirituelle' (*19*, p.48), has become a battleground of ideologies which has destroyed metaphysical and spiritual life and created a world for the most part 'composé d'individus spirituellement, métaphysiquement amputés, handicapés' (*19*, p.49). It is the metaphysical problems fundamental to mankind — those expressed by Bérenger in Act I — which should concern us, while ideologies, in pretending to offer solutions, simply create new and often lethal problems.

Ionesco has been criticized for offering no solution to the spiritual void which surrounds Bérenger at the end. In reply he explained: 'C'est de ce vide qu'un homme libre doit se tirer tout seul, par ses propres forces et non par la force des autres' (*13*, p.292). Only the free individual — free politically and spiritually — can recognize the true problems and attempt to cope with them by upholding human values. It is no answer to bury the problems — and humanity with them — beneath a monstrous lie. Bérenger's essential dilemma is, therefore, not to combat the aberrations of a particular ideology, but to sustain spiritual integrity in the face of mass self-deception.

Ionesco once stated in an interview: 'Il faudrait qu'il y ait un travail constant d'élucidation, de précision, pour abolir "l'absurde" politique... qui est autre que l'absurde fondamental' (*22*, p.139). *Rhinocéros* may be seen as part of that undertaking, as an attempt to demonstrate the absurdity of seeking political answers to the fundamental questions of our existence.

Selective Bibliography

A. WORKS BY IONESCO

(i) Plays

1. *Théâtre I: La Cantatrice chauve, La Leçon, Jacques ou la soumission, Les Chaises, Victimes du devoir, Amédée ou comment s'en débarrasser*, Préface de Jacques Lemarchand, Gallimard, 1954
2. *Théâtre II: L'Impromptu de l'Alma, Tueur sans gages, Le Nouveau Locataire, L'Avenir est dans les œufs, Le Maître, La Jeune Fille à marier*, Gallimard, 1958
3. *Théâtre III: Rhinocéros, Le Piéton de l'air, Délire à deux, Le Tableau, Scène à quatre, Les Salutations, La Colère*, Gallimard, 1963
4. *Théâtre IV: Le Roi se meurt, La Soif et la faim, La Lacune, Le Salon de l'automobile, L'Œuf dur, Pour préparer un œuf dur, Le Jeune Homme à marier, Apprendre à marcher*, Gallimard, 1966
5. *Théâtre V: Jeux de massacre, Macbett, La Vase, Exercices de conversation et de diction françaises pour étudiants américains*, Gallimard, 1974
6. *L'Homme aux valises*, suivi de *Ce formidable bordel*, Gallimard, 1975
7. *Voyages chez les morts: thèmes et variations: Théâtre VII*, Gallimard, 1981

(ii) Editions of *Rhinocéros*

8. *Le Rhinocéros*, Collection Le Manteau d'Arlequin, Gallimard 1959
9. *Rhinocéros*, Collection Folio, Gallimard, 1977 (The edition used here. There are minor amendments to the text of *Théâtre III*.)
10. *Rhinocéros: extraits*, avec une étude méthodique par Claude Abastado, Bordas, 1970 (Contains interesting critical essays and illustrations.)
11. *Rhinoceros: a play in three acts by E. Ionesco*, translated by Derek Prouse, Samuel French, 1960 (An acting edition with production notes.)

(iii) Other works

12. *La Photo du Colonel*, Gallimard, 1962 (A collection of short stories, including the original version of *Rhinocéros* and an autobiographical essay, *Printemps 1939*.)
13. *Notes et contre-notes*, Collection Idées, Gallimard, 1966 (An essential and very readable set of articles on theatre and his own plays. For *Rhinocéros* in particular, see pp.114-22, 277-92.)
14. *Journal en miettes*, Mercure de France, 1967 (Notes on life and literature, accounts of memories and dreams.)

15. *Présent passé Passé présent*, Mercure de France, 1968 (Autobiographical fragments, observations on society and politics.)
16. *Découvertes*, Skira, 1969 (Autobiographical essay, illustrated by the author.)
17. *Le Solitaire*, Mercure de France, 1973 (A novel.)
18. *Antidotes*, Gallimard, 1977 (Miscellaneous articles on literature, politics, etc. For 'rhinoceritis', see pp.93-107.)
19. *Un Homme en question*, Gallimard, 1979 (Miscellaneous articles.)

B. CRITICAL WORKS

(i) Books

20. Abastado, Claude, *Eugène Ionesco*, Bordas, 1971 (A good general introduction, followed by an interview with Ionesco, who tells us why Daisy is only a coquette.)
21. Benmussa, Simone, *Ionesco*, Seghers, 1966 (General introduction, containing Barrault's production notes for the Logician scene.)
22. Bonnefoy, Claude, *Entre la vie et le rêve*, Pierre Belfond, 1977 (Important series of interviews with Ionesco.)
23. Bradesco, Faust, *Le Monde étrange de Ionesco*, Promotion et Edition, 1967
24. Coe, Richard N., *Ionesco*, Oliver and Boyd, 1961 (Despite one or two inaccuracies, this is a good introduction, especially to the ideas behind the drama.)
25. Donnard, Jean-Hervé, *Ionesco dramaturge: ou l'artisan et le démon*, Minard, Lettres Modernes, 1966
26. Frois, Etienne, *Rhinocéros: Ionesco*, Collection Profil d'une œuvre, Hatier, 1970 (A rather brief study.)
27. Pronko, Leonard C., *Eugène Ionesco*, Columbia University Press, 1965 (A brief survey of the plays.)
28. Vernois, Paul, *La Dynamique théâtrale d'Eugène Ionesco*, Préface d'Eugène Ionesco, Klincksieck, 1972 (A very detailed study, with good index and bibliography.)

(ii) Articles and Chapters

29. Autrand, Michel, 'Eugène Ionesco', in *La Littérature en France depuis 1945*, by J. Bersani and others, Bordas, 1970, pp.516-27
30. Duvignaud, Jean, 'La Dérision', *Cahiers Renaud-Barrault*, 29, février 1960, pp.14-22
31. Esslin, Martin, 'Eugène Ionesco: theatre and anti-theatre', in *The Theatre of the Absurd*, Penguin, revised edition, 1968, pp.125-94 (Essential reading.)
32. Fowlie, Wallace, 'New plays of Ionesco and Genet', *The Tulane Drama Review*, 5, September 1960, pp.43-48 (On the Barrault production.)
33. Guicharnaud, Jacques, 'The weight of things: Eugène Ionesco', in *Modern French Theatre from Giraudoux to Genet*, Yale University Press, 1967, pp.215-29

34. Kern, Alfred, 'Ionesco et la Pantomime', *Cahiers Renaud-Barrault*, 29, février 1960, pp.23-26

35. Knowles, Dorothy, 'Eugène Ionesco's Rhinoceroses: their Romanian origin and their Western fortunes', *French Studies*, XXVIII, 3, July 1974, pp.294-307 (Discusses various productions of the play and assesses Ionesco's political stance.)

36. Little, J.P., 'Form and the void: Beckett's *Fin de partie* and Ionesco's *Les Chaises*', *French Studies*, XXXII, 1, January 1978, pp.46-54 (A comparison of the proliferation of objects in Ionesco and Beckett's use of bareness as symbols of the void.)

37. Touchard, Pierre-Aimé, 'Un Nouveau Fabuliste', *Cahiers Renaud-Barrault*, 29, février 1960, pp.3-13 (A most perceptive article.)

C. MISCELLANEOUS WORKS OF REFERENCE

(i) on theatre

38. Boulton, Marjorie, *The Anatomy of Drama*, Routledge and Kegan Paul, 1960

39. Hinchliffe, Arnold P., *The Absurd*, The Critical Idiom, 5, Methuen, 1969

(ii) on the political background

40. Nolte, Ernst, *Three Faces of Fascism*, translated by Leila Vennewitz, New American Library, 1969

CRITICAL GUIDES TO FRENCH TEXTS

edited by
Roger Little, Wolfgang van Emden, David Williams